REVISE EDEXCEL GCSE (9–1)
History
WEIMAR AND NAZI GERMANY, 1918–39

REVISION
GUIDE AND WORKBOOK

Series Consultant: Harry Smith

Author: Victoria Payne

A note from the publisher

In order to ensure that this resource offers high-quality support for the associated Pearson qualification, it has been through a review process by the awarding body. This process confirms that this resource fully covers the teaching and learning content of the specification or part of a specification at which it is aimed. It also confirms that it demonstrates an appropriate balance between the development of subject skills, knowledge and understanding, in addition to preparation for assessment.

Endorsement does not cover any guidance on assessment activities or processes (e.g. practice questions or advice on how to answer assessment questions), included in the resource nor does it prescribe any particular approach to the teaching or delivery of a related course.

While the publishers have made every attempt to ensure that advice on the qualification and its assessment

is accurate, the official specification and associated assessment guidance materials are the only authoritative source of information and should always be referred to for definitive guidance.

Pearson examiners have not contributed to any sections in this resource relevant to examination papers for which they have responsibility.

Examiners will not use endorsed resources as a source of material for any assessment set by Pearson.

Endorsement of a resource does not mean that the resource is required to achieve this Pearson qualification, nor does it mean that it is the only suitable material available to support the qualification, and any resource lists produced by the awarding body shall include this and other appropriate resources.

> **For the full range of Pearson revision titles across KS2, KS3, GCSE, Functional Skills, AS/A Level and BTEC visit:**
> www.pearsonschools.co.uk/revise

Contents

. . . .

A small bit of small print

Edexcel publishes Sample Assessment Material and the Specification on its website. This is the official content and this book should be used in conjunction with it. The questions in *Now try this* have been written to help you practise every topic in the book. Remember: the real exam questions may not look like this.

The legacy of the First World War

The First World War ended in 1918 and left Germany scarred and crumbling, having been defeated by the combined force of Britain, France, Russia, Italy and the USA. Friedrich Ebert, leader of the Social Democratic Party, became the first German president and declared Germany a republic.

What was the impact of the First World War on Germany?

- Two million German troops died and over four million were wounded (11 million in total fought in the war).
- Government debts increased from 50 billion marks to 150 billion marks.
- More than 750 000 Germans died because of food shortages.

The devastating effects of the war left many people with no option other than to revolt by striking and rioting.

The abdication of Kaiser Wilhelm II (the Emperor)

Timeline

- **9 November 1918**
  The Kaiser visited army headquarters in Spa.
- Ministers tried to persuade the Kaiser to abdicate.
- The Kaiser refused.
- Army officers refused to support the Kaiser.
- The Kaiser had no option but to abdicate.

10 November 1918
The Kaiser fled to Holland.

Revolution and the declaration of the republic

Once the Kaiser had abdicated, the German Republic was declared on 9 November 1918.

On 10 November, Friedrich Ebert suspended the old Reichstag and formed the Council of People's Representatives as a temporary measure.

The Berlin streets were crowded. Some people were armed, hoping to take over parts of the city.

Scheidemann talking to the crowds from a window of a house in Berlin, 9 November 1918.

Philipp Scheidemann, of the Social Democratic Party (SDP), the largest party in the German government (Reichstag), declared the new Republic to the crowds. He was fearful that armed rioters were preparing to declare a communist government in Berlin, and, keen to prevent this, he promoted a peaceful transition.

The revolutionary period continued until August 1919, when the Weimar Republic was finally established.

The armistice – the peace agreement between Germany and the Allies

- It was signed on 11 November.
- It was the first major decision of Ebert's new Republic.
- The terms of the peace, the Treaty of Versailles, became a very big burden for the country.

War leaders outside the railway carriage where the armistice was signed on 11 November 1918.

Now try this

Why did the end of the First World War lead to economic and political problems for Germany?

Strengths and weaknesses of the Weimar Constitution

Democratic government was established in the drawing up of a new constitution. This was done on 31 July 1919 in the town of Weimar, rather than in Berlin where there was still unrest.

The Weimar Constitution

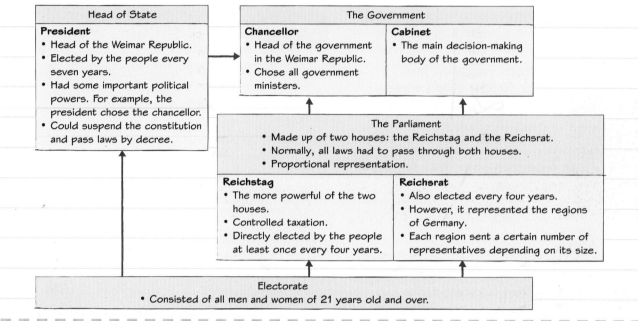

Head of State	The Government	
President • Head of the Weimar Republic. • Elected by the people every seven years. • Had some important political powers. For example, the president chose the chancellor. • Could suspend the constitution and pass laws by decree.	**Chancellor** • Head of the government in the Weimar Republic. • Chose all government ministers.	**Cabinet** • The main decision-making body of the government.

The Parliament
• Made up of two houses: the Reichstag and the Reichsrat.
• Normally, all laws had to pass through both houses.
• Proportional representation.

Reichstag	Reichsrat
• The more powerful of the two houses. • Controlled taxation. • Directly elected by the people at least once every four years.	• Also elected every four years. • However, it represented the regions of Germany. • Each region sent a certain number of representatives depending on its size.

Electorate
• Consisted of all men and women of 21 years old and over.

Strengths and weaknesses of the Weimar Constitution

Strengths	Weaknesses	
• Proportional representation made sure small parties had a fair share of seats. • Women able to vote as well as men. • Voting age reduced from 25 to 21. • No one group or person could have too much power. • There was an election for president every seven years. • Central government was more powerful than before, but local government still retained power in the regions. • The Reichsrat could regulate the power of the Reichstag by delaying new laws.	• Proportional representation led to coalition governments that were unstable, or found it difficult to have strong policies and often fell apart. • Lack of strong government led to weakness in a crisis that ended up with the president passing laws without the prior consent of the Reichstag. Article 48 of the constitution enabled the president to do this. • It was not the choice of the people so was not that popular.	**Frauen!** Gleiche Rechte – Gleiche Pflichten **Wählt sozialdemokratisch!** SOZIALDEMOKRATISCHE PARTEI DEUTSCHLANDS. A poster encouraging women to vote for the SDP and proclaiming equal rights and obligations.

Now try this

Describe the key strengths and the key weaknesses of the new constitution.

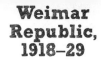

Why the Republic was unpopular

The Treaty of Versailles damaged Germany's economy making the Weimar Republic weak from the start. People blamed the leaders of the new German republic for signing it. They were labelled the 'November Criminals' because they surrendered in November 1918 and were seen as traitors to their country.

Article 231 of the Treaty of Versailles said that Germany was guilty of starting the war. Ordinary German people hated this blame and felt very resentful because of it. They believed they fought the war in self-defence and that other countries were to blame. These people are demonstrating in Leipzig against the treaty.

The treaty and reparations

As the war guilt clause made Germany accept the blame for the war, the Allies said they were entitled to reparations (compensation). £6600 million was to be paid in yearly instalments to the Allies to repair damage in their countries.

The treaty and military forces

- ✔ Army limited to 100 000.
- ✔ Navy limited to six battleships, six cruisers, 12 destroyers and 12 torpedo boats (and no submarines).
- ✔ All planes were destroyed and no air force was allowed.
- ✔ No military was allowed in the land bordering France (the Rhineland).

The treaty and land losses

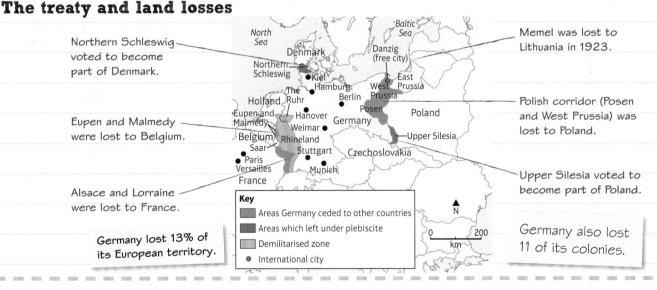

Northern Schleswig voted to become part of Denmark.

Eupen and Malmedy were lost to Belgium.

Alsace and Lorraine were lost to France.

Germany lost 13% of its European territory.

Memel was lost to Lithuania in 1923.

Polish corridor (Posen and West Prussia) was lost to Poland.

Upper Silesia voted to become part of Poland.

Germany also lost 11 of its colonies.

Key
- Areas Germany ceded to other countries
- Areas which left under plebiscite
- Demilitarised zone
- ● International city

0   200
km

The 'stab in the back' theory

Many German people never believed their army had been defeated in the war. Those who criticised the treaty said that the army had been betrayed by politicians – that they were 'stabbed in the back' and forced to surrender when they could have won.

Now try this

Write an acrostic poem to sum up why the Treaty of Versailles was so unpopular with the German people. Try using the word 'Versailles' as your base word.

Remember, an acrostic poem is when the first letters of each line spell out a phrase.

Challenges from left and right

The new Weimar Republic government faced opposition from groups inside and outside the Reichstag, and from both the left and right wings.

The Spartacists

- ✓ Left-wing
- ✓ Came from the Independent Socialist Party
- ✓ Had backing from the Soviet Union
- ✓ Led by Rosa Luxemburg and Karl Liebknecht
- ✓ Based in Berlin

The Freikorps

- ✓ Right-wing
- ✓ Made up of ex-soldiers who had kept their weapons
- ✓ Had 250 000 men in March 1919
- ✓ Organised by regular army

Challenge from the left – the Spartacist Revolt

In January 1919, the Spartacists took over the government's newspaper and telegraph bureau, and tried to organise a general strike in Berlin. The Weimar government sent Freikorps units to put down the revolt.

There was street fighting in Berlin for several days before the revolt ended and Spartacist leaders were shot.

Challenge from the right – the Kapp Putsch

In March 1920, Freikorps troops, fearing unemployment, decided to march on Berlin. Ebert asked the head of the army to resist the Freikorps but he refused. A nationalist politician, Dr Wolfgang Kapp, was put in charge by the rebels and the Weimar government fled Berlin seeking safety. In order to put down the rebels, or Kapp Putsch as it became known, the government organised the trade unions to go on strike. This they did and the national strike caused such chaos that Kapp could not rule Germany and was forced to flee. The Weimar ministers returned.

Political attacks on the Weimar Republic

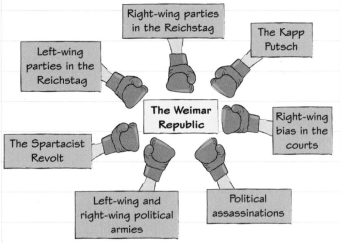

Right-wing parties in the Reichstag

The Kapp Putsch

Left-wing parties in the Reichstag

The Weimar Republic

Right-wing bias in the courts

The Spartacist Revolt

Left-wing and right-wing political armies

Political assassinations

Political assassinations

- From 1919–1923 politicians in the Weimar Republic were worried about assassinations.
- In the early years of the republic, 376 political assassinations took place.
- Some right-wing extremists used the murders to weaken the new republic.
- Conservative judges were sympathetic to the conservative cause and gave them light punishments.

Now try this

Describe the role of the Freikorps in the Kapp Putsch and the Spartacist Revolt.

The challenges of 1923

In 1923 the German people faced a terrible economic crisis. There was hyperinflation that made the German currency worthless.

Hyperinflation

When the price of goods increases it is called inflation; when it increases spectacularly, it is called hyperinflation.

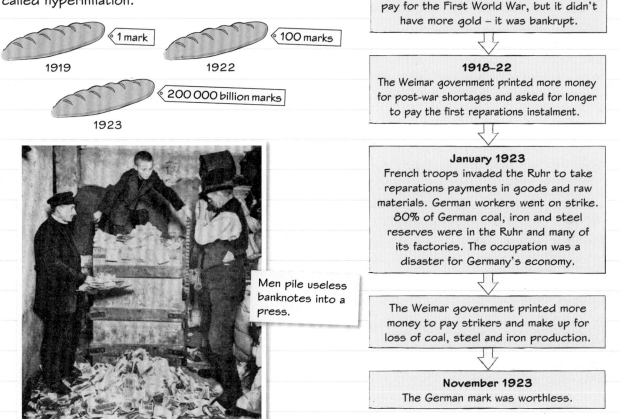

◁ 1 mark
1919

◁ 100 marks
1922

◁ 200 000 billion marks
1923

Men pile useless banknotes into a press.

Why there was hyperinflation

1914–18
The government printed more money to pay for the First World War, but it didn't have more gold – it was bankrupt.

⬇

1918–22
The Weimar government printed more money for post-war shortages and asked for longer to pay the first reparations instalment.

⬇

January 1923
French troops invaded the Ruhr to take reparations payments in goods and raw materials. German workers went on strike. 80% of German coal, iron and steel reserves were in the Ruhr and many of its factories. The occupation was a disaster for Germany's economy.

⬇

The Weimar government printed more money to pay strikers and make up for loss of coal, steel and iron production.

⬇

November 1923
The German mark was worthless.

The effects of hyperinflation

Negative effects
- 👎 Some people could not afford essentials like bread.
- 👎 Wages rose, but not as quickly as prices.
- 👎 Some businesses went bankrupt. (Those that made money took over the struggling ones.)
- 👎 People with fixed or monthly incomes, such as pensioners, suffered most.
- 👎 Savings became worthless. This affected the middle classes most.
- 👎 People blamed the Weimar government, which made it even more unpopular.

Positive effects
- 👍 Farmers benefited, as they were paid more for food.
- 👍 Some people and businesses could pay off loans and mortgages.
- 👍 Fixed rents for rooms or shops became very cheap.
- 👍 Foreign visitors could buy more for their money.

Now try this

Make a list of all the ways in which Germany was affected by hyperinflation.

Include the groups or types of person most affected.

The effects of hyperinflation on Germany are important for understanding various topics, so make sure you revise them.
- Remember that middle-class people were worst affected.
- Include positive and negative effects of hyperinflation in your list.

Reasons for recovery, 1923–29

From 1923–29 Germany managed to recover from the immediate crisis of 1923, but there were still significant weaknesses in its economy. Gustav Stresemann, the new chancellor, played an important role.

Rentenmark

✓ In November 1923, Stresemann set up the Rentenbank and issued the new currency called the Rentenmark.

✓ Supply of these notes was tightly controlled. Their value was tied to the price of gold so it had real value. This encouraged more public confidence.

✓ In August 1924 the Reichsbank was given control of this new currency. It was renamed the Reichsmark. Hyperinflation was over.

The Reichsmark provided a much stronger basis for the recovery of jobs and businesses, but it could not bring back the losses experienced in the hyperinflation crisis.

International loans after the First World War

loans made under Dawes Plan and Young Plan

USA → Germany

war loans paid back ← reparations payments made

Britain and France

The Dawes Plan, 1924

In 1924, Charles Dawes, an American banker, designed a plan so Germany could pay its reparations.

- Instalments were temporarily reduced to £50 million a year.

- US banks agreed to make loans to German industry. The Allies felt more confident that they would get their reparations payments.

Gustav Stresemann (far left) at the London conference in 1924, where the Dawes Plan was agreed.

Young Plan, 1929

In August 1929, a committee, set up by the Allies and led by an American banker called Owen Young, proposed a plan.

👍 The Young Plan reduced the total reparations debt from £6.6 billion to £2 billion.

👍 The payments could be made over a longer time, up until 1988.

👍 Lower reparations meant lower taxes for German people.

👎 There was a lot of opposition, especially from the extreme political parties, like the Nazis, who felt it was extending the burden for future generations.

Improvements in the economy

The Weimar Republic's economy improved because:

👍 industrial output doubled by 1928 and finally passed pre-First World War levels

👍 employment and trade increased.

However, there were still problems.

👎 The extreme political parties were completely against Germany paying the reparations at all.

👎 The economic recovery depended on American loans, so it remained fragile.

Now try this

Write a paragraph to explain how the German economy was still vulnerable, despite improvements.

Stresemann's success at home and abroad

Stresemann's most important achievements were in economic and foreign policy. However, his main aim was to stabilise the political situation in Germany.

Stresemann's success

Gustav Stresemann resigned the chancellorship in November 1923, but stayed as foreign secretary until 1929. His work in foreign affairs:

- ✓ strengthened the confidence of the German people in the Weimar Republic
- ✓ reduced the support for extremist political parties like the Nazis and the communists
- ✓ increased support for moderate parties
- ✓ reduced the economic hardships of the German people.

Stresemann was instrumental in making sure Germany was a member of three important international pacts or agreements: The Locarno Pact, the League of Nations and the Kellogg-Briand Pact.

Locarno Pact 1925

This was an agreement between Germany, Britain, France, Italy and Belgium. In it:

- Germany agreed to its new border with France improving relations with the French
- the Allies and Germany agreed to the permanent demilitarisation of the Rhineland
- German membership of the League of Nations was up for discussion.

Why was it a success for Germany?

- It improved relations with France with the border agreement.
- The Locarno Pact was not imposed on Germany, unlike the Treaty of Versailles.
- It increased the status and popularity of the Weimar Republic.
- It helped boost confidence in more moderate political parties.

League of Nations

This was a new international body that hoped to discuss world problems in order to avoid war. It was set up in 1920 but Germany was initially excluded. In 1926, they were invited to join and they became a member of the council.

Why was it a success for Germany?

- It showed that Germany's views counted.
- It boosted the confidence held by most Germans in the Weimar government.

Kellogg-Briand Pact 1928

This was an agreement between 62 nations. It committed countries to avoiding the use of war to achieve foreign policy objectives.

Why was it a success for Germany?

- It showed that Germany was once again a major power.
- It showed that moderate political parties could build Germany's strength internationally.
- It increased public confidence in how Germany was being led.

It wasn't all a success

There were still some areas of discontent in spite of Stresemann's work.

- The hated terms of the Treaty of Versailles were still in place.
- The League of Nations was, for some, a symbol of the unpopular Treaty of Versailles.
- Some didn't like the confirmation of the new border with France.
- There were still extremist parties around.

Think about Stresemann's position, his achievements and their results.

Now try this

Explain how Stresemann's foreign policy helped to stabilise Germany.

Changes for workers and women

The period 1924–29 saw some important improvements for workers and women in Germany, but there were still underlying problems in German society.

Changes in living standards

Living standards improved after 1924, brought about by government funding and policies.

Unemployment insurance

👍 3% of workers' earnings were deducted to be put towards insurance that would give them a basic amount of benefits if they became unemployed or sick.

Wages and work

👍 Working hours reduced.

👍 Wages rose.

👍 Working conditions improved.

👎 Hyperinflation made employment insecure.

👎 Well-off Germans resented seeing workers benefiting.

Standard of living

Housing

👍 15% rent tax was introduced to fund building associations.

👍 Between 1925 and 1929, 101 000 homes were built.

👎 There was still a housing shortage but things had improved.

Women at work	Women at leisure	Women in politics
• Some of the gains in equality brought about by the war were lost. • Most women gave up work after they married. There was a drop in women working from 75% in 1918 to 36% in 1925. • Few women secured high status jobs. • There was an increase in part-time work. • Some professions, like teaching and medicine, offered new opportunities to women. • Women were encouraged to go to university.	• Greater earning power led to more independence for younger, single women. • Women were less interested in marriage and family and more interested in having a 'good time'. • The behaviour of 'new women' was not liked by some men and women who felt traditional values were being eroded.	• Women earned the vote in 1918 and could stand for elections. • 90% turned out at elections. • Article 109 of the constitution stated that women had equal rights with men and could enter professions on an equal basis. • Marriage was an equal partnership.

Now try this

For each of the following groups in Germany between 1924 and 1929, give **one** example of progress and **one** example of lack of progress: a) workers b) women.

Cultural changes, 1924–29

A variety of factors led to a rise in cultural changes and experimentation in Germany between 1924 and 1929. The main driving force in art and cinema was the movement called Expressionism.

Art

Weimar artists painted everyday life so that everyone could have access to their art. They wanted to make art that commented on problems in German society, or to make people think. Their style of work was called Expressionism, which was concerned with raw emotion, the seedier side of everyday life and confronting the disaster of the First World War. Artists like Otto Dix and George Grosz were influential to the movement, as was Paul Klee.

Cave Flowers by Paul Klee, 1926. Klee taught at the Bauhaus school.

Cinema

Films became popular all over the world in the 1920s. Expressionism flourished in film-making, particularly in Weimar Germany due to fewer restrictions. Some German films were very new and exciting in how they challenged traditional cinema.

Science Fiction
Metropolis
Directed by Fritz Lang

Horror
THE CABINET OF DR. CALIGARI
Directed by Robert Wiene

Ghost story
The Cat and the Canary
Directed by Paul Leni

All these films were marked by dark shadows, dramatic lighting and grotesque characters.

A famous and very popular German actress of the time was Marlene Dietrich. Here she is in the film *The Woman One Longs For*, directed by Curtis Bernhardt in 1929.

Architecture

New designers and architects challenged traditional ideas and practices in building and interiors.

The Bauhaus school was set up in Weimar, in 1919, by the architect Walter Gropius.

Gropius wanted to bring together all the disciplines (art, architecture, design, typography, sculpture, etc).

The Bauhaus School in Dessau designed by Gropius, 1925–26.

The school attracted many talented artists and designers.

Their ideas challenged traditional styles that had been popular before the war.

Their approaches looked radical compared to what had come before.

Now try this

How did the new Weimar culture challenge traditional attitudes and values in Germany?

Hitler and the early growth of the party

Adolf Hitler was born in Austria in 1889. He moved to Munich in 1913 and became obsessed with all things German. He fought in the First World War and his experience confirmed his views that Germany had a special destiny. He was shocked by Germany's defeat and the outcome of the Treaty of Versailles.

Hitler and the early DAP/NSDAP

Timeline

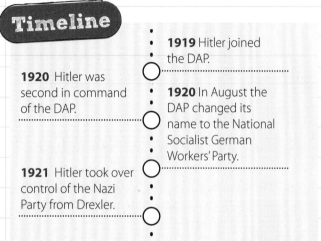

1919 Hitler joined the DAP.

1920 Hitler was second in command of the DAP.

1920 In August the DAP changed its name to the National Socialist German Workers' Party.

1921 Hitler took over control of the Nazi Party from Drexler.

Hitler's early political career

1. The German Worker's Party (DAP) was set up by Anton Drexler in February 1919, in Munich; Hitler joined in September 1919.

2. The DAP set up permanent headquarters, Hitler became second in command.

3. Hitler suggested a new name for the party – the National Socialist German Workers' Party (NSDAP) or NAZI Party for short.

4. In July 1921, Hitler became leader of the Nazi Party.

5. Hess, Goering, Streicher and Röhm were selected as some of his party supporters.

The 25-point programme

The Nazi programme, written by Hitler and Drexler in 1920, included the following points.

- Increase pensions for the elderly.
- Nationalise industries.
- Get rid of the Treaty of Versailles.
- Everybody should have a job.
- Build up Germany's armed forces.
- Only German races may be members of the nation. No Jew may be a citizen.
- Expand Germany across new territory to feed the people and to settle surplus population (known as Lebensraum).
- All citizens should have equal rights and duties.
- Every hard-working German to have the chance of higher education.
- State must protect mothers and infants, stop children working; make laws for compulsory sports.

The programme opposed: the Weimar politicians who agreed to the Treaty of Versailles; democracy, which they thought was weak; and Jews, who they felt undermined the German economy.

The Sturmabteilung (SA)

The Sturmabteilung (or stormtroopers) were a paramilitary force, made up of unemployed ex-soldiers. They were formed in August 1921 by Hitler and put under the command of Ernst Röhm. They wore brown uniforms and were nicknamed 'Brownshirts'. They were used to disrupt opposition meetings and to control crowds and any opposition to Hitler – often violently.

The Sturmabteilung

Now try this

Choose **three** Nazi policies from the 25-point programme and explain to whom they would have appealed and why.

10

The Munich Putsch and its aftermath

Hitler attempted to overthrow the Weimar government in November 1923. This was known as the Munich Putsch. After this date, and up to 1928, the Nazi Party struggled to get support.

Reasons for the Munich Putsch

Long term	Medium term	Short term
• 'Stab in the back' • Reparations • The loss of Germany's colonies. • Resentment of Weimar government, particularly by the Bavarian government.	Hitler was influenced by Mussolini's right-wing party in Italy – the Fascists. Mussolini marched on Rome in 1922, forcing the democratic government to accept him as leader.	• Hyperinflation • French troops entered Ruhr in 1923 and took over German businesses. • Hitler thought that he had support.

The events of the Putsch

Timeline

9 November 1923
Hitler gathered with 1000 SA and 2000 volunteer supporters and marched on Munich town centre to declare himself President of Germany. The group was met by state police. Someone opened fire and there was chaos. Ludendorff, Röhm and Streicher were arrested.

8 November 1923
Hitler with 600 SA entered a beer hall in Munich where the Bavarian government were meeting.
At gunpoint, Hitler forced government leaders to support him.
Röhm took over local police and army headquarters.
Ludendorff, behind Hitler's back, let the government leaders go.

11 November 1923
Hitler was found hiding at a friend's house and was arrested.

SA storming Munich town centre

Consequences of the Putsch

In the short term, the Putsch was not good for Hitler. He was in prison and the NSDAP was banned, and the Putsch had failed miserably because of lack of support.
In the long term, however, the consequences were more positive for Hitler and the NSDAP.

• Hitler used his trial to publicise his views.

• He used his time in prison to write *Mein Kampf* (*My Struggle*). This book became a bestseller when published – it outlined his political ideas and in particular his views on Jews.

• The events of the Putsch made Hitler realise that the party needed to rethink its tactics and be more organised in order to win support nationally, using violence and force wasn't enough.

Hitler was released from prison after only nine months. The ban on the NSDAP was lifted by 1925.

Bamberg Conference 1926

Hitler organised this conference to address splits between the socialist and nationalist wings of the Nazi movement. Hitler's power as leader was secured and his vision of Nazism taken forward.

Now try this

Design **two** mind maps to sum up the reasons for and consequences of the Munich Putsch.

Growth in support, 1929–32

In this period, the Nazis reorganised to benefit from the Weimar Republic's weaknesses and economic problems. Hitler's appeal as a leader also benefited them.

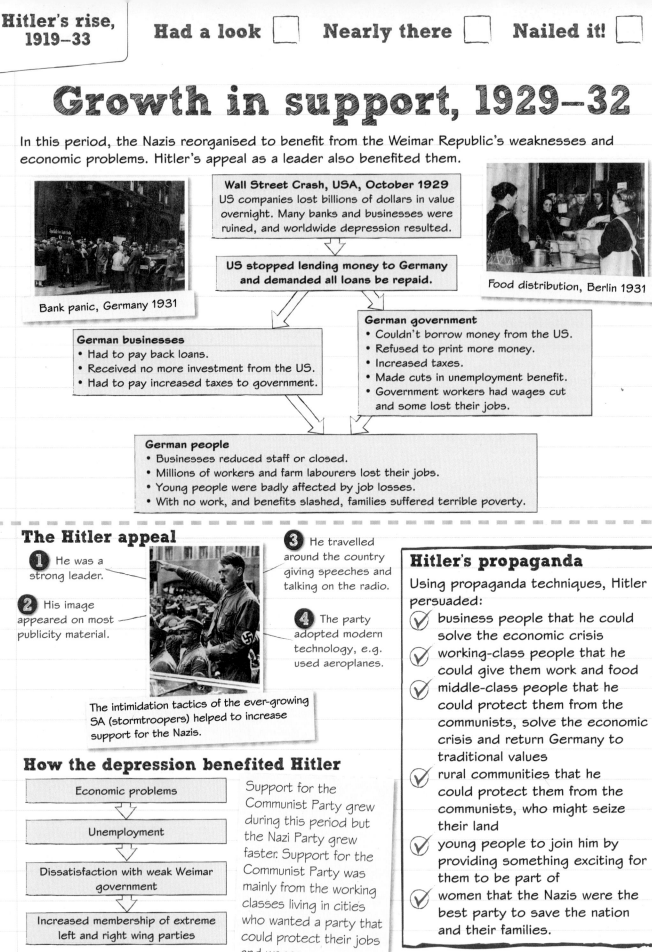

Bank panic, Germany 1931

Wall Street Crash, USA, October 1929
US companies lost billions of dollars in value overnight. Many banks and businesses were ruined, and worldwide depression resulted.

Food distribution, Berlin 1931

US stopped lending money to Germany and demanded all loans be repaid.

German businesses
- Had to pay back loans.
- Received no more investment from the US.
- Had to pay increased taxes to government.

German government
- Couldn't borrow money from the US.
- Refused to print more money.
- Increased taxes.
- Made cuts in unemployment benefit.
- Government workers had wages cut and some lost their jobs.

German people
- Businesses reduced staff or closed.
- Millions of workers and farm labourers lost their jobs.
- Young people were badly affected by job losses.
- With no work, and benefits slashed, families suffered terrible poverty.

The Hitler appeal

1 He was a strong leader.

2 His image appeared on most publicity material.

3 He travelled around the country giving speeches and talking on the radio.

4 The party adopted modern technology, e.g. used aeroplanes.

The intimidation tactics of the ever-growing SA (stormtroopers) helped to increase support for the Nazis.

How the depression benefited Hitler

Economic problems
↓
Unemployment
↓
Dissatisfaction with weak Weimar government
↓
Increased membership of extreme left and right wing parties

Support for the Communist Party grew during this period but the Nazi Party grew faster. Support for the Communist Party was mainly from the working classes living in cities who wanted a party that could protect their jobs and wages.

Hitler's propaganda

Using propaganda techniques, Hitler persuaded:
- ✓ business people that he could solve the economic crisis
- ✓ working-class people that he could give them work and food
- ✓ middle-class people that he could protect them from the communists, solve the economic crisis and return Germany to traditional values
- ✓ rural communities that he could protect them from the communists, who might seize their land
- ✓ young people to join him by providing something exciting for them to be part of
- ✓ women that the Nazis were the best party to save the nation and their families.

Now try this

Complete a table listing the reasons for the rise of the Nazis in one column and the problems of the Weimar Republic in the other.

Remember that, until the economic problems after 1929, the Nazis had very little success in elections.

Political developments in 1932

The actions of four key people resulted in Hitler becoming Chancellor. You will need to know who these people were and the sequence of political events.

The four key players

Paul von Hindenburg – hero of the First World War and President of the Weimar Republic.

Heinrich Brüning – the Chancellor.

General Franz von Papen – the politician and friend of Hindenburg.

Kurt von Schleicher – the army general.

Paul von Hindenburg

Heinrich Brüning

Kurt von Schleicher

General Franz von Papen

Hitler's road to power

Timeline

May 1932
Election with Hindenburg being re-elected as President. Hitler increases his share of the vote.
Chancellor Brüning bans the SA and announces a plan to buy up land from landowners and use this to house the unemployed. Both plans are very unpopular and Brüning resigns.
Brüning is replaced by von Papen – he is put forward by von Schleicher.
Von Schleicher had been planning a coalition between right-wing supporters and the Nazis.
Hitler agrees to the coalition if the ban on the SA is removed.
The coalition takes power.

November 1932
Further election.
Von Schleicher warns Hindenburg that if von Papen stays as Chancellor there will be civil war.
Von Papen goes.

January 1933
Von Schleicher does not have the support of the public or the Nazis.
He persuades Hindenburg that he could be the head of a military dictatorship.
Hindenburg refuses.
Von Papen persuades Hindenburg to appoint Hitler as Chancellor to avoid von Schleicher's military dictatorship. He also suggests that he should become Vice-Chancellor so that he can keep a check on Hitler.
Hitler becomes Chancellor.

April 1932
Hindenburg stands for re-election as President. No one party has 50% of the vote.

July 1932
Further elections take place – there is widespread fighting between the communists and the Nazis.
The Nazi share of the vote increases from 18% in 1930 to 38%.
Hitler demands that he be made Chancellor – Hindenburg refuses.

December 1932
Von Schleicher becomes Chancellor.

Now try this

1 Write down the reasons why Hitler was able to become Chancellor.
2 Number them in order of importance, from least to most important.

Causes that are more important often have an effect on other causes.

The Reichstag Fire and the Enabling Act, 1933

Now the Nazis and Hitler were in power, they used every opportunity, legal and illegal, to remove any opposition and secure a dictatorship.

The Reichstag Fire

1 A lone Dutch communist was executed for starting the fire but Hitler seized the opportunity to accuse the Communist Party of a conspiracy against the government. Four thousand communists were arrested.

2 It gave Hitler an excuse to issue a Decree for the Protection of the People and the State, giving him powers to imprison political opponents and ban opposition newspapers.

3 He persuaded Hindenburg to call an election in March 1933 to secure more Nazi seats.

4 The Nazi Party managed to secure two-thirds of the seats by using the emergency powers to prevent the communists from taking up their 81 seats.

5 Hitler was now able to change the constitution.

The Reichstag Fire of 27 February 1933. Marinus van der Lubbe was arrested and killed for starting the fire – some people believed the Nazis had started the fire deliberately.

The Enabling Act, 1933

Hitler proposed the Enabling Act in order to destroy the power of the Reichstag and give himself total power to make laws. It stated that:

☑ the Reich Cabinet could pass new laws

☑ the laws could overrule the constitution

☑ Hitler would propose the laws.

Result: Germany would no longer be a democracy.

Hitler expected resistance to the act and so used the SA to intimidate the opposition. The vote was won by the Nazis 444 to 94.

The effect the Enabling Act had on trade unions and political parties

The Enabling Act allowed Hitler to get rid of opposition to the Nazis.

Local Government: this was closed down on 31 March 1933 and reorganised with Nazi majorities. It was completely abolished in January 1934.

Trade unions: these were replaced with the German Labour Front. Many union officials were arrested on 2 May 1933.

Other political parties: in May 1933, the SDP and Communist Party offices and funds were taken by the Nazis. In July 1933, other political parties were banned.

Now try this

Summarise the events of the Reichstag Fire and what followed.

Hitler becomes Führer

Hitler continued to assert his authority and power. Key events occurred in 1934 which led to Hitler declaring himself Führer.

Röhm, Hitler and the SA

Röhm did not like Hitler's policies.

The leaders of the Schutzstaffel (SS) wanted to reduce the size of the SA in order to increase their own power.

Why Röhm and the SA were a threat to Hitler

Many of the SA were bitter because they felt undervalued and angry because many were still unemployed, but they were loyal to Röhm.

The SA was much bigger than the army and the army feared Röhm wanted to replace them.

The 'SS'

The SS was set up by Hitler in 1925 to act as his bodyguards. They were a select group run firstly by Schreck and then by Himmler. They appeared menacing in their black uniforms.

SS troops guarding Hitler as he makes a speech, May 1934.

The Night of the Long Knives

Hitler decided to rid himself of the threat of Röhm and the SA. He did this by inviting Röhm and 100 SA leaders to a meeting in the town of Bad Wiessee on 30 June 1934. It was a ruse – when the leaders arrived they were arrested by the SS, taken to Munich and shot.

After the arrests, von Papen's staff were arrested and his home surrounded. Von Papen was no longer able to watch what Hitler was up to. Further killings occurred, including that of von Schleicher.

It was thought that not many people fully realised how many people were being killed – many were relieved that the power of the SA had been curtailed.

Death of Hindenburg

President Hindenburg was the only person senior to Hitler. In August 1934, he died. Within hours, a Law Concerning the Head of State merged the offices of Chancellor and President to create a new office of Führer.

Führer means 'leader' and Hitler used propaganda to ensure that he looked all powerful. The 'Heil Hitler!' Nazi salute made people swear loyalty to him personally, and he was portrayed as having superhuman, heroic qualities.

Army oath of allegiance

The day Hindenburg died, Hitler announced the army should swear an oath of allegiance to him, not to Germany.

Now try this

Write a paragraph to explain the steps Hitler took in 1934 to secure his power in Germany.

A police state

A police state is when a government uses the police to control everyone's lives. The Nazis used the SS, SD and the Gestapo to do this. Anyone the Nazis were suspicious of could disappear, at any time. They could be killed or taken to concentration camps.

Policing

Hitler set up his own security forces as he realised not all the existing German police supported him. These forces were run by the Nazi Party, not by the government. Their main weapon was fear.

SS (Protection Squad)
- Set up by Heinrich Himmler in 1925.
- They were led by Himmler.
- They wore black uniforms.
- They controlled all Germany's police and security forces.
- They acted outside the law.
- Members had to marry 'racially pure' wives.
- They ran the concentration camps.

SD (Security Service)
- Set up by Heinrich Himmler in 1931.
- They were led by Reinhard Heydrich.
- They wore uniforms.
- Spied on all opponents of the Nazi Party, both at home and abroad.

Gestapo (Secret State Police)
- Set up by Hermann Goering in 1933.
- They were led by Reinhard Heydrich.
- They wore plain clothes.
- They spied on people.
- Prosecuted people for speaking out against the Nazis.
- Sent people to concentration camps and used torture.

The legal system

Hitler controlled the legal system so that meant it was very difficult for anyone to oppose him. He did this by controlling the judges.

- All judges had to belong to the National Socialist League for the Maintenance of the Law.
- All judges had to favour the Nazi Party in any decision.

He also did this by controlling the law courts.

- He abolished trial by jury – only judges were able to decide whether someone was innocent or guilty.
- He set up a People's Court to hear all treason cases. Trials were held in secret and judges were hand-picked.

Concentration camps up to 1939

The first camp was built at Dachau in 1933 to house the growing number of people being arrested.

Dachau concentration camp in 1933.

Camps were built in isolated areas so no one could see what was going on. Many more were built.

Inmates were made up of:
- political prisoners
- undesirables, such as prostitutes and homosexuals, and minority groups like Jews.

Inmates were treated very badly and forced to do hard labour.

Now try this

Jot down **three** ways in which the SS was used to control the German people.

Any answer about how the Nazis controlled Germany should feature the SS.

Policies towards the churches

The Nazis wanted total loyalty to Hitler and his beliefs. The churches were potentially a threat to his power and therefore Hitler needed to control the churches' influence.

Nazi vs Christian beliefs

Nazi beliefs	Christian beliefs
Hitler as all-powerful leader.	God as the ultimate authority.
Aryan racial superiority.	Everyone equal in the eyes of God.
War, military discipline and violence important.	Peace is what everyone should strive for.
Dominance of the strong over the weak.	The strong should look after the weak.

The Catholic Church

Hitler worried that the Catholic Church would oppose him because Catholics:

- were loyal to the pope
- usually supported the Catholic Centre Party
- sent their children to Catholic schools and the Catholic youth organisation.

The Concordat

In July 1933, Hitler agreed with the pope in a Concordat that Catholics were free to worship and run their own schools in return for staying out of politics. However, Hitler broke his promise and:

- priests opposing the Nazis were harassed and/or sent to concentration camps
- Catholic schools had to remove Christian symbols and were later closed
- Catholic youth organisations were banned.

By 1937, the pope spoke out against Hitler in his statement known as 'With Burning Anxiety', which criticised Nazi policies.

Hitler's strategy was to try and consolidate his power before openly attacking the influence and power of the churches in Germany. His ultimate goal was to replace the churches with a Nazi-based religion.

For more information on churches in the Nazi period, see page 19.

The Protestant churches

Two Protestant churches were formed during the 1930s.

1 The Reich Church:

- was founded in 1933
- was made up of about 2000 Protestant churches
- supported the Nazis
- was led by Ludwig Müller
- had some members that wore Nazi uniform and called themselves German Christians.

SA troops outside a pro-Nazi church service, July 1933.

2 The Confessional Church:

- was founded in 1934
- was made up of about 6000 Protestant churches
- opposed the Nazis
- was led by Martin Niemöller
- was repressed by the Nazis.

For more on Martin Niemöller see page 19.

Now try this

1 List **three** ways that the churches cooperated with the Nazis.
2 List **three** ways that the churches resisted the Nazis.

17

Propaganda and censorship

Hitler wanted to use propaganda (information to spread ideas) and censorship (government control over what people see, hear and read) to create a generation of people loyal to the Nazi regime and its values.

Joseph Goebbels – Reich Minister of Propaganda 1933–1945

Goebbels played a central role as Nazi Minister of Enlightenment and Propaganda. He was a master at spreading Nazi ideas in a subtle as well as an unsubtle way. He essentially controlled newspapers, the radio, book publishing, film and the arts.

Methods of censorship

- ✓ Public burning of books by Jewish writers or others who disagreed with Nazi views.
- ✓ Radio producers, playwrights, filmmakers and newspapers were told what to say.
- ✓ Newspapers opposing the Nazis were closed.
- ✓ Only radios that couldn't receive foreign stations were made.

Methods of propaganda

Hitler featured in much propaganda, either with a photograph or his name or title.

Posters showing Nazi beliefs were displayed everywhere.

Huge rallies and military parades were held, projecting a power and strength that would either make Germans proud of their country or fill them with terror depending on their viewpoint.

The cinema showed propaganda films, but mainly entertainment films that had subtle Nazi messages.

Hitler made radio speeches which were played through loudspeakers in factories, cafés and on the streets. Entertainment programmes contained Nazi ideas and beliefs.

The Nazis encouraged artists and playwrights to produce work highlighting Nazi ideas. 'Degenerate' art, such as modern art and jazz music, was banned.

The Olympic games held in Berlin in 1936 was the ideal event to promote Nazi ideologies such as Aryan superiority. It was also an opportunity to present Nazi Germany in a good light. It was well organised and a grand spectacle.

The Reich Chamber of Culture

Set up in 1933 and overseen by Goebbels, this monitored all aspects of culture and made sure they were consistent with Nazi ideas. The Nazis wanted grand and classical architecture, particularly the work of Albert Speer; artists to be members of a Reich Chamber of Visual Arts; to listen to traditional German composers like Beethoven and Bach.

Now try this

Write down **one** method of propaganda that targeted each of the following groups in Germany: workers, women and young people.

Church opposition

The extent of support for the Nazi regime differed between groups and individuals. Although Hitler tried to suppress opposition from the churches, there were still Catholic priests and Protestant ministers and pastors who preached against Nazi policies.

Pastor Martin Niemöller

One of the main church opponents of Hitler was Martin Niemöller, but he didn't always oppose the Nazis.

Niemöller's changing attitude to Hitler.

Pro-Nazi

- Niemöller voted for them in the 1924 and 1933 elections as he felt the Weimar Republic needed a strong leader.
- He didn't oppose Nazi restrictions on Jews.
- He wanted to be let out of prison to fight on the side of the Nazis in the Second World War.

Against Nazis

- He didn't like Nazi interference in the Protestant Church.
- He opposed the Nazi restrictions on Jews becoming Christians.
- He set up the Confessional Church in 1934.

Very against Nazis

- Niemöller was arrested many times for speaking out against the Nazis and Hitler between 1934 and 1937.
- He was sent to a concentration camp in 1938 where he stayed until 1945.

For more on the Confessional Church, see page 17.

How pastors and priests opposed the Nazis

- 6000 Protestant pastors joined Niemöller's Confessional Church as a protest against Nazi policy, only 2000 remained in the German Christian Church.
- About 800 pastors were arrested and sent to concentration camps.
- 400 Catholic priests spoke out and were arrested and imprisoned in the Priests' Block at Dachau concentration camp.

Niemöller sermon

Niemöller preached this sermon to remind church leaders of the importance of speaking out against Nazi policies.

First they came for the Socialists,
and I did not speak out
because I was not a Socialist.
Then they came for the Trade Unionists,
and I did not speak out
because I was not a Trade Unionist.
Then they came for the Jews,
and I did not speak out
because I was not a Jew.
Then they came for me
and there was no one left to speak for me.

Martin Niemöller

How much opposition was there?

Opposition to the Nazis by church leaders was difficult because it was so dangerous to speak out openly. However, attendance at Christian churches remained high throughout the period, in spite of the Nazis' attempt to curtail the churches.

Pastor Martin Niemöller preaching

Now try this

Why couldn't Hitler gain complete control of the churches?

Youth opposition

Another group that opposed the Nazis was the young. Some young people set up secret groups or refused to conform to what the Nazis wanted from them.

The Edelweiss Pirates

A group of Edelweiss Pirates in 1938.

They sang 'Smash the Hitler Youth in twain, our song is freedom, love and life'.

The Nazis were not threatened by their activities.

They were made up mainly of boys who copied an American style of clothing (checked shirts and white socks).

By 1939 they had 2000 members.

They were formed in the late 1930s, possibly as a consequence of Nazi policies enforcing Hitler Youth membership.

They went on hikes and camping expeditions in the countryside to get away from Nazi restrictions.

The Alpine flower, the edelweiss, was used as their symbol.

They taunted the Hitler Youth.

They were mainly based in working-class districts of large cities.

They read and listened to banned music and literature and wrote anti-Nazi graffiti.

For more on the Hitler Youth, see page 22.

The Swing Youth

Another group of young people similar to the Edelweiss Pirates was the Swing Youth. Like the Pirates, they chose not to conform to Nazi ideas. They liked wearing American clothes. They listened to American music and watched American films. They gathered to drink alcohol, smoke and dance. They organised illegal dances attended by thousands. Unlike the Pirates they were largely made up of children from wealthy families with the money to buy records and own record players.

How effective was youth opposition up to 1939?

It was limited to:

- writing anti-Nazi graffiti
- telling anti-Nazi jokes
- attacking the Hitler Youth
- listening to banned music
- wearing American-style clothing.

A 1930s portable gramophone on which records would have been played.

The motives of the youth opposition groups were cultural rather than political and their numbers were limited.

Now try this

List **three** ways that young people resisted the Nazis.

Women and the family

The Nazis had strong views about the role and position of women in society. Once they had control in Germany, they introduced policies that affected women's lives in lots of ways.

The Nazis' ideal woman

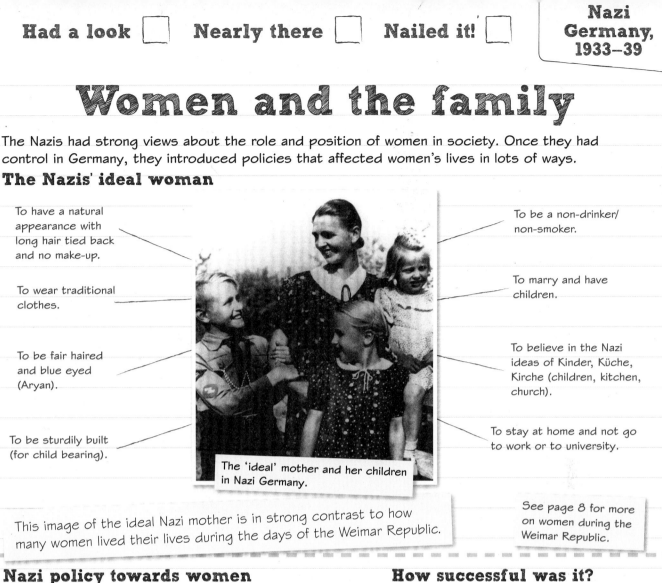

To have a natural appearance with long hair tied back and no make-up.

To wear traditional clothes.

To be fair haired and blue eyed (Aryan).

To be sturdily built (for child bearing).

To be a non-drinker/non-smoker.

To marry and have children.

To believe in the Nazi ideas of Kinder, Küche, Kirche (children, kitchen, church).

To stay at home and not go to work or to university.

The 'ideal' mother and her children in Nazi Germany.

This image of the ideal Nazi mother is in strong contrast to how many women lived their lives during the days of the Weimar Republic.

See page 8 for more on women during the Weimar Republic.

Nazi policy towards women

Nazi policy towards women	How successful was it?
Women should not work, especially those who were married. Many professional women lost their jobs and were replaced by men.	During 1933–36 the number of employed married women fell.
Women should get married. The Marriage Law of 1933 initiated the use of vouchers (Marriage Loans) to newly married couples if the woman agreed to stop working.	The number of marriages did increase, but it's not clear if this was due to Nazi policy, or to other reasons such as a stronger economy.
Women should have at least four children. (Couples were let off one-quarter of their Marriage Loan repayments for each child they had.)	The birth rate did increase, but this may have been because the economy was improving rather than because of Nazi policies. Few women had more than two children.
The German Women's Enterprise gave women medals for having children, and ran classes and radio programmes on home-based matters.	The German Women's Enterprise had six million members, which suggests that many women welcomed Nazi policies.

Now try this

Write down **three** differences between women's roles in Weimar Germany and Nazi Germany.

Don't forget to look back at page 8 to answer this question.

Nazi youth organisations

There were four Nazi youth groups: Young German Folk (boys aged 10–14), Young Girls (girls aged 10–14), Hitler Youth (boys aged 14–18), and League of German Maidens (girls aged 14–18). Meetings and activities took place after school, at weekends and in the holidays.

Nazi aims for young people

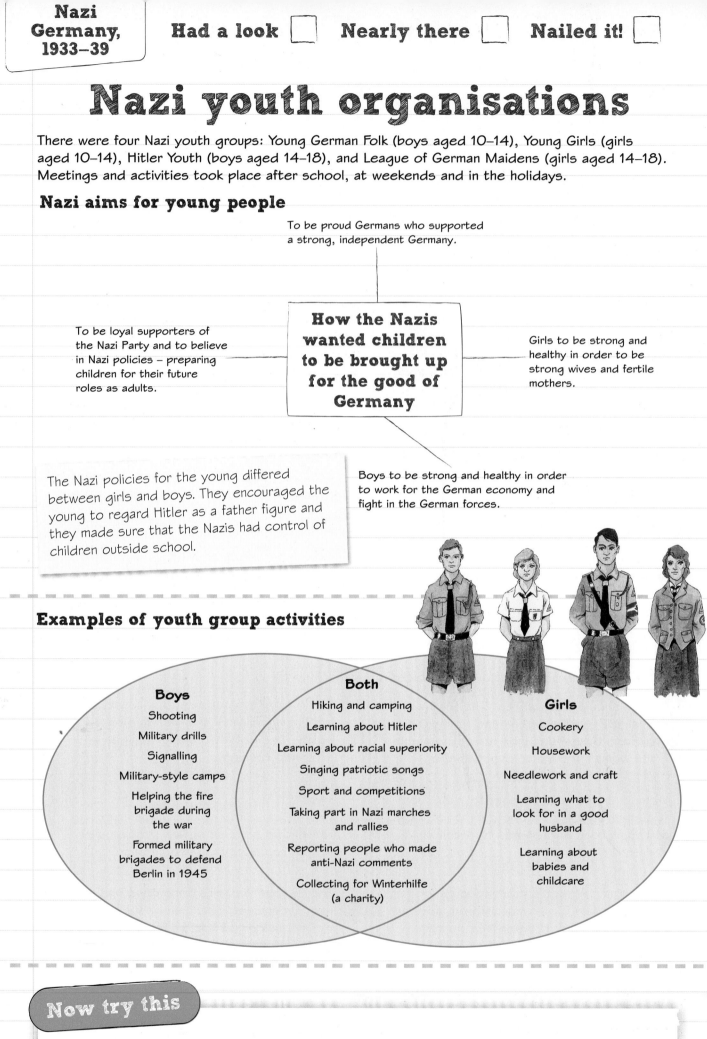

To be proud Germans who supported a strong, independent Germany.

How the Nazis wanted children to be brought up for the good of Germany

To be loyal supporters of the Nazi Party and to believe in Nazi policies – preparing children for their future roles as adults.

Girls to be strong and healthy in order to be strong wives and fertile mothers.

The Nazi policies for the young differed between girls and boys. They encouraged the young to regard Hitler as a father figure and they made sure that the Nazis had control of children outside school.

Boys to be strong and healthy in order to work for the German economy and fight in the German forces.

Examples of youth group activities

Boys
- Shooting
- Military drills
- Signalling
- Military-style camps
- Helping the fire brigade during the war
- Formed military brigades to defend Berlin in 1945

Both
- Hiking and camping
- Learning about Hitler
- Learning about racial superiority
- Singing patriotic songs
- Sport and competitions
- Taking part in Nazi marches and rallies
- Reporting people who made anti-Nazi comments
- Collecting for Winterhilfe (a charity)

Girls
- Cookery
- Housework
- Needlework and craft
- Learning what to look for in a good husband
- Learning about babies and childcare

Now try this

Why did Hitler force young people to join the Nazi youth groups?

Nazi education

Another way the Nazis controlled children was through education. This was another method of making German children loyal Nazis in preparation for their future roles in the Nazi state.

Nazi control of education

Schools	Teachers	Subjects	Propaganda
• Children had to attend state school until they were 14. • There were separate schools for girls and boys. • Optional schools after age 14: National Political Educational Institutes and Adolf Hitler Schools. • All schools followed a set curriculum – this was different for girls and boys.	• It was compulsory for teachers to be Nazi Party members. • Those who didn't teach Nazi ideas were dismissed. • Teachers' camps taught them how to use Nazi ideas in their teaching. • Nearly all teachers joined the Nazi Teachers' League. • Teachers were forced to attend courses to learn about Nazi ideas.	• 15% of time was spent on PE to ensure a healthy and strong population. • Girls were taught domestic skills, while boys were taught science and military skills. • Both sexes were taught the traditional subjects: German, History, Geography and Maths. • New subjects: Race Studies and Nazi Eugenics were taught to both sexes.	• All lessons began and ended with the Hitler salute. • Nazi flags and posters decked classrooms. • From 1935 all textbooks had to be approved by the Nazi Party. • Traditional subjects were rewritten to glorify Germany, e.g. an emphasis on German writers and historical figures. • Racial ideas and anti-Semitism were embedded within subjects.

Race Studies involved learning how to classify racial groups and about the superiority of the Aryan race. Eugenics is the science of using controlled breeding to attempt to produce the perfect human being.

The ultimate aim of the Nazi education policy

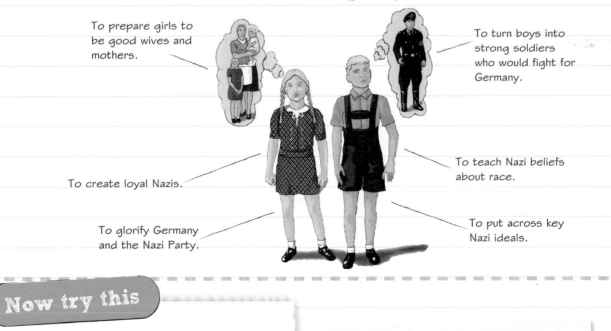

To prepare girls to be good wives and mothers.

To turn boys into strong soldiers who would fight for Germany.

To create loyal Nazis.

To teach Nazi beliefs about race.

To glorify Germany and the Nazi Party.

To put across key Nazi ideals.

Now try this

Explain why the Nazis made the education of boys and girls different.

Think about the aims of Nazi education as well as the content of the lessons.

23

Policies to reduce unemployment

Reducing the high levels of unemployment was important for Hitler. From 1933 he set out schemes to achieve this.

Why Hitler wanted to get people working

The unemployed:

1 were dangerous politically - if they were poor and hungry they might turn to other political parties for help.

2 were believed by the Nazis to be a burden on society and a waste of valuable resources.

National Labour Service (RAD)

This was started by the Weimar government and continued by the Nazis.

- From July 1935, it was compulsory for all men aged 18–25 to serve for six months on this scheme.
- They worked on job creation schemes and other public works such as draining marshes.
- Many hated RAD: the pay was low, the hours long and the work boring.

Job creation schemes

The Nazis reduced unemployment by putting money into large projects. These benefited the economy and also reduced unemployment.

7000 km of autobahns (motorways) connecting up the country.

Public buildings.

Construction projects

Sports facilities, e.g. stadia for the Berlin Olympics, 1936.

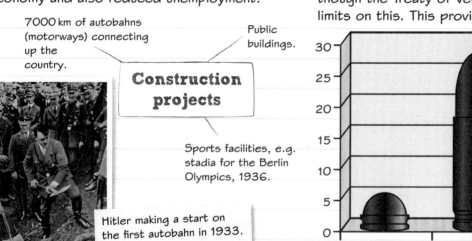

Hitler making a start on the first autobahn in 1933.

Rearmament

Another way that the Nazis provided jobs was through building up their stockpile of arms, even though the Treaty of Versailles had stipulated limits on this. This provided many jobs.

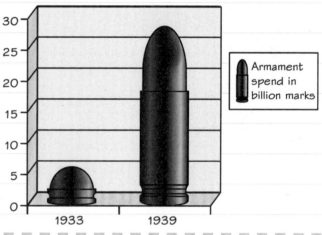

Armament spend in billion marks

Invisible unemployment

Official government figures showed unemployment was falling but they did not include:

- Jews being forced out of jobs
- women being dismissed or leaving their jobs
- unmarried men under 25 doing National Labour Service
- opponents of the regime who were sent to concentration camps.

Official figures showed that unemployment had dropped from 4.8 million in 1933 to 0.3 million in 1939 – an amazing achievement. But this did not take into account 'invisible unemployment'.

Now try this

Who benefited from the Nazi employment policies and who didn't?

Think about 'invisible unemployment'.

The standard of living

Nazi economic policies, in general, improved the standard of living of the German people, although some sectors of society lost out.

Nazi workers' organisations

Hitler realised that he must make sure that the German workers were satisfied and avoid losing their support. He set up different workers' organisations that were meant to improve the lives and conditions of German people.

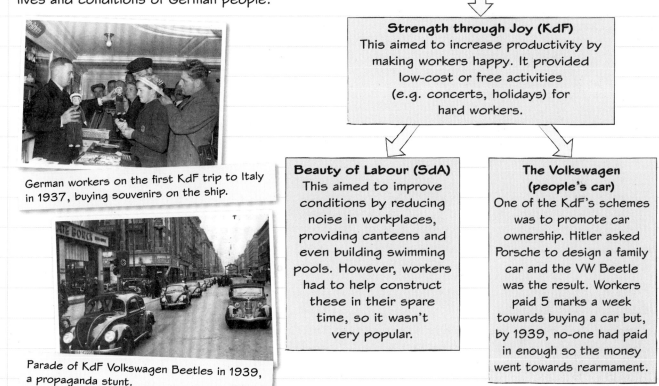

German workers on the first KdF trip to Italy in 1937, buying souvenirs on the ship.

Parade of KdF Volkswagen Beetles in 1939, a propaganda stunt.

German Labour Front
The Deutsche Arbeitsfront (DAF) replaced trade unions. Workers had to be members. It ran several schemes.

↓

Strength through Joy (KdF)
This aimed to increase productivity by making workers happy. It provided low-cost or free activities (e.g. concerts, holidays) for hard workers.

Beauty of Labour (SdA)
This aimed to improve conditions by reducing noise in workplaces, providing canteens and even building swimming pools. However, workers had to help construct these in their spare time, so it wasn't very popular.

The Volkswagen (people's car)
One of the KdF's schemes was to promote car ownership. Hitler asked Porsche to design a family car and the VW Beetle was the result. Workers paid 5 marks a week towards buying a car but, by 1939, no-one had paid in enough so the money went towards rearmament.

Had the standard of living improved by 1939?

Better off	Worse off
👍 More jobs with most men in work.	👎 'Invisible unemployment' meant many were still unemployed.
👍 Average wages rose by 20% compared to 1933.	👎 The cost of food rose by an equivalent amount so this cancelled out the wage rise.
👍 KdF provided leisure activities and holidays and SdA improved working conditions.	👎 With the banning of trade unions, workers had few rights and worked longer hours: 43 hours a week in 1933 up to 49 hours in 1939.
👍 Car ownership increased three-fold.	👎 Only high earners could afford cars. Low earners had to spend money on essentials.

Now try this

Decide whether you think the standard of living of the German people had improved by 1939, or not, then write a paragraph backing up your decision.

Racial beliefs and policies

Hitler was keen to increase the number of 'pure' Germans (Aryans) who were blond-haired, blue-eyed, tall and athletic, and who would work hard, join the army or have children.

Nazi racial hierarchy

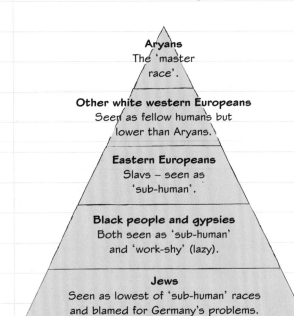

Aryans
The 'master race'.

Other white western Europeans
Seen as fellow humans but lower than Aryans.

Eastern Europeans
Slavs – seen as 'sub-human'.

Black people and gypsies
Both seen as 'sub-human' and 'work-shy' (lazy).

Jews
Seen as lowest of 'sub-human' races and blamed for Germany's problems.

How the race grew

'Race farms' were set up where Aryan men and women met to have Aryan children. The SS were central to the Nazi master race, as they only recruited Aryans and were only allowed to marry Aryan women.

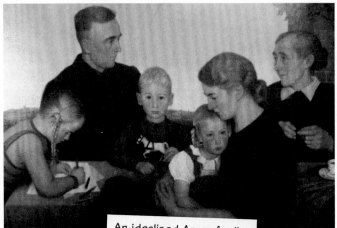

An idealised Aryan family.

Untermenschen

Untermenschen meant 'inferior people' or 'sub-humans', and was the term used by Nazis to describe Slavs, gypsies, black people and Jews.

- In 1935, the Nuremberg Laws banned Aryans from marrying gypsies, black people or Jews.
- Mixed-race children were sterilised.
- After 1933, many gypsies were arrested and sent to concentration camps. From 1938, all gypsies had to be registered and were banned from travelling. In 1939, they were told they would be deported.
- Slavs were reminded continually that they didn't fit the Aryan ideal, but were persecuted less than other groups.

For more on the Nuremberg Laws and treatment of Jews, see pages 27 and 28.

Other undesirables

The Nazis also believed other groups of society were undesirable and should be treated differently.

- Homosexuals were sent to prison or concentration camps and subjected to medical experiments to correct their 'disorder' after laws against homosexuality were strengthened.
- Mentally handicapped people were sterilised after a new law, The Prevention of Hereditarily Diseased Offspring was introduced in 1933.
- Mentally and physically handicapped babies were killed.
- Vagrants were seen as 'work shy' and put in concentration camps.

Now try this

Describe how the Nazi policies on race became harsher as the 1930s wore on.

⟵ The treatment of gypsies is a good example to use.

Jewish persecution 1

The persecution of the Jewish community in Germany escalated throughout this period. It began with an attack on Jewish businesses and the removal of Jewish people from their jobs.

Associated with communism (Karl Marx was Jewish).

Jealous of their success – many Jews were professionals or owned businesses.

Long-standing distrust of Jewish people – a common belief across Europe.

Reasons why Jews were persecuted

Used as scapegoats for Germany's problems.

Suspicious of a different religion.

Blamed for Germany's defeat in First World War and the Treaty of Versailles (especially as some politicians involved were Jewish).

Reasons why most non-Jewish German people let the persecution happen

The influence of Nazi anti-Semitic propaganda.

The fear of the Gestapo and SS if they did speak out.

Jewish businesses

Timeline

1933 The SA organised a one-day boycott of Jewish shops. They painted a yellow star on doors and discouraged people from going inside.

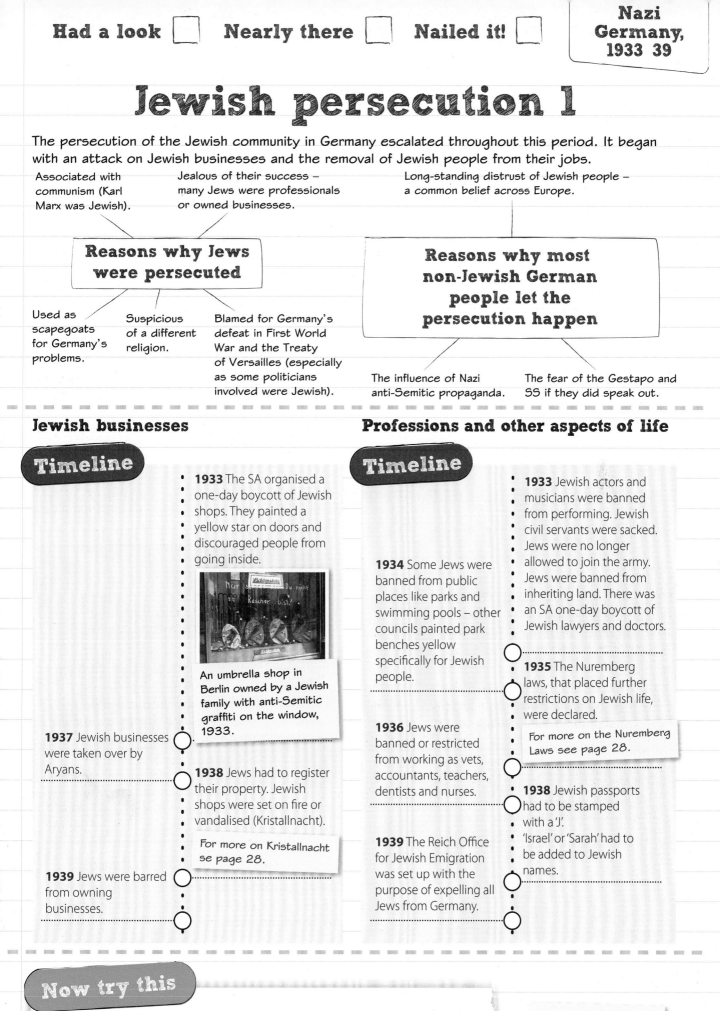

An umbrella shop in Berlin owned by a Jewish family with anti-Semitic graffiti on the window, 1933.

1937 Jewish businesses were taken over by Aryans.

1938 Jews had to register their property. Jewish shops were set on fire or vandalised (Kristallnacht).

For more on Kristallnacht se page 28.

1939 Jews were barred from owning businesses.

Professions and other aspects of life

Timeline

1933 Jewish actors and musicians were banned from performing. Jewish civil servants were sacked. Jews were no longer allowed to join the army. Jews were banned from inheriting land. There was an SA one-day boycott of Jewish lawyers and doctors.

1934 Some Jews were banned from public places like parks and swimming pools – other councils painted park benches yellow specifically for Jewish people.

1935 The Nuremberg laws, that placed further restrictions on Jewish life, were declared.

For more on the Nuremberg Laws see page 28.

1936 Jews were banned or restricted from working as vets, accountants, teachers, dentists and nurses.

1938 Jewish passports had to be stamped with a 'J'. 'Israel' or 'Sarah' had to be added to Jewish names.

1939 The Reich Office for Jewish Emigration was set up with the purpose of expelling all Jews from Germany.

Now try this

Describe **three** different types of persecution experienced by the Jewish community. You could describe economic persecution, social persecution and open violence.

You could use details from page 28 as well.

Jewish persecution 2

Two events occurred during this time that had a major impact on the lives of Jewish communities in Germany. These were the passing of the Nuremberg Laws and the terrifying events of Kristallnacht.

The Nuremberg Laws, 1935

A new set of laws was passed to make it easier to persecute Jews.

The Reich Law on Citizenship
- Only those of German blood can be citizens.
- Jews must become subjects not citizens.
- Jews cannot vote or work for the government.
- Jews must wear a yellow star-shaped patch sewn on clothes for ease of identification.

The Reich Law for the Protection of German Blood and Honour
- No Jew must marry a German citizen.
- No Jew is allowed to have sexual relations with a German citizen.

Hitler at the Nuremberg Rally where the Laws were declared.

Kristallnacht (the Night of the Broken Glass), 1938

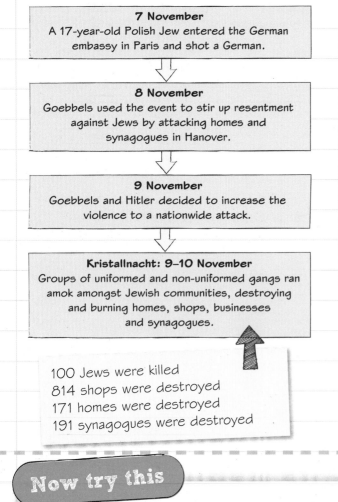

7 November
A 17-year-old Polish Jew entered the German embassy in Paris and shot a German.

⬇

8 November
Goebbels used the event to stir up resentment against Jews by attacking homes and synagogues in Hanover.

⬇

9 November
Goebbels and Hitler decided to increase the violence to a nationwide attack.

⬇

Kristallnacht: 9–10 November
Groups of uniformed and non-uniformed gangs ran amok amongst Jewish communities, destroying and burning homes, shops, businesses and synagogues.

100 Jews were killed
814 shops were destroyed
171 homes were destroyed
191 synagogues were destroyed

A Berlin shop destroyed during Kristallnacht, 1938.

Consequences of Kristallnacht

Goebbels blamed the Jews for starting the trouble on Kristallnacht and ordered them to pay damages. Jews were fined 1 billion marks.

Now try this

Discuss how the Nuremberg Laws and Kristallnacht were a turning point in the treatment of Jews in Nazi Germany.

Exam overview

This page introduces you to the main features and requirements of the Paper 3 Option 31 exam paper.

About Paper 3

- Paper 3 is for your modern depth study.
- Weimar and Nazi Germany, 1918–39 is a modern depth study and is Option 31.
- It is divided up into two sections: Section A and Section B. You must answer **all** questions in both sections.
- You will receive two documents: a question paper, which you write on, and a Sources/Interpretations Booklet, which you will need for section B.

 The Paper 3 exam lasts for 1 hour 20 minutes (80 minutes). There are 52 marks in total. You should spend approximately 25 minutes on Section A and 55 minutes on Section B.

Links You can see examples of all six questions on pages 31–36 and in the practice questions on pages 38–49.

The questions

The questions for Paper 3 will always follow this pattern:

Section A: Question 1
Give two things you can infer from Source A about...   **(4 marks)**

Complete the table.

Question 1 targets AO3 (analysing, evaluating and using sources to make judgements). Spend about six minutes on this question, which focuses on **inference** and **analysing** sources. Look out for the key term 'infer'.

Section A: Question 2
Explain why...   **(12 marks)**

Two prompts and your own information.

Question 2 targets both AO1 (showing knowledge and understanding of the topic) and AO2 (explaining and analysing events using historical concepts such as causation, consequence, change, continuity, similarity and difference). Spend about 18 minutes on this question.

Section B: Question 3(a)
How useful are Sources B and C for an enquiry into...?   **(8 marks)**

Use the sources and your knowledge of the historical context.

Question 3(a) also targets AO3. Spend about 12 minutes on this question, which is about **evaluating the usefulness** of contemporary sources.

Section B: Question 3(b)
Study Interpretations 1 and 2...

What is the main difference between these views?   **(4 marks)**

Use details from both interpretations.

Questions 3(b) and 3(c) target AO4 (analysing, evaluating and making judgements about interpretations). Spend about six minutes on each of these questions, which are about **suggesting and explaining why** the interpretations differ.

Section B: Question 3(c)
Suggest **one** reason why Interpretations 1 and 2 give different views about...   **(4 marks)**

You can use the sources provided to help explain your answer.

Section B: Question 3(d)
How far do you agree with Interpretation 1/2 about...? **(16 marks + 4 marks for SPaG and use of specialist terminology)**

Use both interpretations and your knowledge of the historical context.

Question 3(d) also targets AO4. Spend about 30 minutes on this question, which is about **evaluating** an interpretation. Up to 4 marks are available for **spelling, punctuation, grammar (SPaG)** and use of specialist terminology.

Sources and interpretations

This exam asks you to analyse and evaluate both sources and interpretations, and you need different skills for each.

Questions 1 and 3(a)

Here you will be asked to look at sources. These sources could be propaganda posters, accounts from people at that time, photographs or any written or visual source that is **from the period**. As the sources are generated from that time it is helpful to think about the nature of the source, the origin, who produced it, and the purpose for which it was produced.

Questions 3(b), (c) and (d)

Here you will be asked to read interpretations of a particular enquiry or event from two different historians. Unlike analysing sources, interpretations are written **after the time period or event**. They are often written by historians or commentators who express their views and opinions about historical people, events and changes. As they are people's views and judgements based on evidence there can be differences, and sometimes clear disagreements, about what people think.

Content: what information can you get directly from the source and its caption? It is important to spend time reading and studying sources before you read the exam questions.

Bias: a source is still useful even if you think it is biased – it can be good for assessing people's opinions of an event, for example.

Nature: what type of source is it – a diary entry, newspaper article, cartoon? This will help you to assess reliability, usefulness and purpose.

Language: in written sources, the author's language should give you clues about whether they are biased or even unreliable. Using appropriate examples by quoting directly from the source will help you gain better marks. Language can also tell you about the purpose of a source.

Hints and tips for examining sources

Origins: the caption should tell you who produced the source and when. The origin will help you assess its reliability, usefulness and purpose.

Purpose: the reason a source was created could be one of the questions by itself, but this will also help you to assess its reliability and usefulness.

Selection: what has the author / artist chosen to include? What have they chosen to leave out? It's important to consider both of these when you are thinking about the reliability, usefulness and purpose of a source.

Hints and tips for analysing and evaluating interpretations

How complete?	How objective?	What is the chosen emphasis?
The interpretations can be different because they are concerned with finding out about different aspects of the enquiry and may cover different ground. Sometimes, historians set out to look at one aspect specifically, whereas others may want to look at related issues in a broader sense.	Historians can hold different views because they come from a particular school of thought. Therefore, their questions and answers are shaped by their wider views of society and how it works and has worked in the past. This can have an important impact on the judgements and opinions they hold about historical matters.	Sometimes, historians use the same sources but reach different views because they place a different level of importance on the same evidence. They may have access to the same material sources as each other, but will draw different conclusions about the significance of that evidence.

Question 1: Making inferences

Question 1 on your exam paper will ask you to 'infer from source A...'. There are 4 marks available for this question.

Source A: A poster used during the Berlin Olympics in 1936.

Making inferences from a source

Making inferences is working something out that isn't directly shown. First of all, think about what is suggested or implied by the source and then try to show how the source helped you make that inference. Include supporting details from the source to back up what you say.

Worked example

Give **two** things you can infer from Source A about propaganda in Nazi Germany.

Complete the table below to explain your answer.

(4 marks)

 **Links** You can revise Nazi propaganda on page 18.

Sample answer

(i) What I can infer:
That Hitler wanted to use the Olympic games to show the world how strong the Nazi regime was.
Details in the source that tell me this:
The predominance of the Swastika flag; the strength and fitness of the athlete and the signs of industry in the background.
(ii) What I can infer:
That the games have been organised by the Nazi regime.
Details in the source that tell me this:
The Swastika flags behind the athlete and on the athlete's vest show that the athlete supports the Nazi regime and is happy to represent it.

You must consider the intended audience and the purpose for which the source was produced. Also, think about when it was produced as this context is vital for analysing the source, not just describing it.

Sometimes, it is helpful to think about what you can see and then move on to think about what it **suggests**. You need to make sure that you don't just describe the source but go further and show you can make inferences.

Question 2: Explaining causes

Question 2 on your exam paper will ask you to 'Explain why...'. There are 12 marks available for this question.

Worked example

Explain why the Nazis wanted women to focus on home and family life. **(12 marks)**

You may use the following in your answer:

* Marriage Loans
* birth rate.

You **must** also use information of your own.

🔗 **Links** You can revise the role of women on page 21.

Explaining key features and causes

Explaining why involves looking at the key features of something and thinking about its causes. Key features are accurate and relevant knowledge. Causes are what led to a situation or change happening. To explain causes, you must show how a number of causes led to that event or change.

You **must** use your own knowledge and not limit yourself to the bullet points.

Sample answer

The Nazis wanted women to stay at home and look after a large family so the population would grow.

The Nazis believed that women and men had different roles in society. This meant that women were expected to follow traditional ideas about the importance of caring for children.

Here the student has given a correct cause but only a vague answer, and hasn't developed an explanation.

This is also a correct cause and the beginning of an explanation: the student needs to add more detail to the explanation to improve this answer.

Improved answer

The Nazis wanted the population of Germany to grow so they tried to limit women to roles within the home and family. After the First World War, Germany's population had been falling and Hitler was keen to expand Germany so it was vital to make sure women had more children. They were given special medals to reward them for having large families, which included bronze, silver and gold if you had over eight children. There were also financial incentives for women, such as Marriage Loans. The 1933 Law for the Encouragement of Marriage lent couples money when they married, if the wife left work. For each child they had, they were let off a quarter of this loan. These policies show how the Nazi government encouraged women to focus on their family and raising children.

Another important cause was Hitler's ideas about 'racial purity'. He was determined to increase the number of Aryan children and reduce the number of non-Aryans and minority groups in Germany. The Nazi policies on women gave encouragement to Aryan mothers, but other minority groups were stopped from having children by being sterilised.

Make sure you identify what reasons led to the Nazis making women focus on home and family.

This states the cause and explains why the Nazis wanted to restrict women to the home and family.

This student has used their knowledge of the period to support their answer with specific examples.

🔗 **Links** The information about the Marriage Law shows use of relevant knowledge. Revise these Nazi policies on page 21.

Using 'Another important cause was...' to introduce a new point is a good way of writing a clear answer.

You could also include some information about how the League of German Maidens prepared young women for their future roles.

Question 3(a): Evaluating usefulness

Question 3(a) on your exam paper will ask you to judge 'How useful are sources B and C...'. There are 8 marks available for this question.

Worked example

Study Sources B and C on page 37.

How useful are Sources B and C for an enquiry into why people supported the Nazis?

Explain your answer, using Sources B and C and your knowledge of the historical context.   **(8 marks)**

Judging usefulness of sources

To judge the usefulness of a source, you need to think about the enquiry question and the criteria you will use to reach your decision. You will need to consider the **provenance** of each source – its nature, origin and purpose – and whether these make the source useful or not in addressing the enquiry question.

Sample answer

He was a member of the Nazi Party and was very keen, 'I committed myself, body, soul and spirit'. He knew what it felt like to be part of the organisation and he shows how people could have got swept away in the excitement.

The poster is useful because it shows the Nazis wanted to get support from different groups, like women. They used posters to try to get support for the Nazis in the elections in the early 1930s.

This answer lacks analysis and describes rather than judges the usefulness of the sources.

🔗 **Links** For more information, see pages 16, 18 and 22–24.

Improved answer

The Nazi Party member is recollecting his feelings about joining and supporting the Nazi Party. He describes his circumstances as unemployed, possibly in the early 1930s when unemployment reached a new high in Germany. He is quite defensive about his support for the party and says an outsider would 'not understand'. His personal experience of the emotions tied up in his membership are useful to understand the emotional appeal that the Nazis drew on to build support, but could also be a limitation as he is clearly concerned about how people in hindsight might view him and his support for the Nazis when he was a young man.

The poster is useful for finding out about why different groups supported the Nazis. It gives us insight into how the Nazis targeted different groups with specific messages. In this case, women are urged to consider their roles as wives and mothers in order to rally their support. However, the poster in isolation does not help us judge the impact of the poster on the audience, just the messages that the Nazi Party wanted to convey in order to gain support. The women who did vote Nazi were probably swayed by these ideas as the Nazis wanted to make women believe that their role in the home and family was valuable and they wanted them to accept a different gender role to men.

This student has used criteria about origins and audience in judging the usefulness of this source for the enquiry.

Key terms

Provenance – the origin of a source.
Nature – what type of source it is, such as a propaganda poster or a speech extract.
Purpose – the reason a source was created.

Specific language is used in this answer, such as: insight, judge, impact, convey, promote.

This answer is a good answer because it evaluates the poster for this enquiry by considering its **nature** and **purpose** and it highlights issues about the impact on the audience.

Question 3(b): Identifying and explaining differences

Question 3(b) on your exam paper will ask you to identify 'the main difference between the views' in two interpretations. There are 4 marks available for this question.

Worked example

Study Interpretations 1 and 2 on page 37. They give different views about the German public's support for the Nazis.

What is the main difference between the views?

Explain your answer, using details from both interpretations. **(4 marks)**

Remember to include points from both sources. It's important to refer directly to the interpretation and include short quotations to support what you say.

Spotting and explaining differences in interpretations

An interpretation is a historian's account or explanation based on evidence. When analysing the differences between interpretations, think about the points of view the historians present. Look for the important or key differences, not just the surface details. For this question you need to look for a fundamental difference that you can spot.

 Links For more information on the German public's support for the Nazis, see pages 12, 14–16.

Sample answer

These interpretations are different because the first one says that the Gestapo heard everything, whereas the second historian says that some crimes were reported to the regular police, not the actual Gestapo.

This answer focuses on a surface point of difference rather than the underlying difference. A stronger answer would pick out a more fundamental difference.

This student uses short quotations to support the analysis.

Improved answer

Delarue argues that the Gestapo achieved 'comprehensive penetration' of German society. Therefore, the attitudes of the German public were fully controlled by the Gestapo. He claims the use of 'terror and horror' was successful in making sure that the public believed the Gestapo was all-knowing and 'overheard' all activities or even the smallest action. On the other hand, Rees states that the Gestapo's work in controlling people's attitudes was based more on a public willingness to cooperate with them, rather than due to terror. He backs this up by saying that 80% of political crimes investigated by the Gestapo were as a result of 'ordinary citizens', rather than Nazi Party members denouncing people and reporting their 'suspicions' to the Gestapo.

The focus of this answer is on the key point of difference, rather than more minor differences.

Here, a key difference is explained and supported with detailed points from both interpretations.

You must think about the specific language you can use in your answer, like: 'argues', 'claims', 'states', 'on the other hand' and 'backs this up'. These phrases help you produce a better answer because they help show you are analysing another person's judgement or opinion about something.

Question 3(c): Suggesting reasons for different views

Question 3(c) on your exam paper will ask you to explain why two interpretations give different views. There are 4 marks available for this question.

Worked example

Suggest **one** reason why Interpretations 1 and 2 on page 37 give different views about German public support for the Nazis.

You may use Sources B and C on page 37 to help explain your answer.   **(4 marks)**

 **Links** You can revise public support for the Nazis on pages 12, 14–16.

You must give **one** reason why historians reach different conclusions about historical questions.

'Suggest' questions

In a question that asks you to suggest a reason, you need to offer and explain an idea about why there are differences. For example, interpretations might differ because they give different weight to different sources, because they aren't complete extracts, or because the authors have a different emphasis or focus. You need to show you understand that historical interpretations are judgements and opinions based on evidence and that, as a result, different views can exist.

Sample answer

One reason Interpretations 1 and 2 give different views is that the historians have different focuses.

In Interpretation 1, Delarue focuses on the role of the Gestapo, discussing the widespread atmosphere of terror the organisation created, rather than asking wider questions about the support the Nazis received from the German public.

In contrast, in Interpretation 2, Rees examines how the German public gave their support to the Nazi regime. Rees suggests that ordinary German people may have cooperated willingly rather than because they felt intimidated.

This idea is supported by Source B, which shows how long-term unemployment and the disillusionment this created were also possible reasons for Nazi support.

In this answer, the student explains the different views in the interpretations by looking at the different focuses the historians have chosen.

The explanation in this answer is clear and refers to **both** interpretations.

The student has used Source B to back up their argument about why the interpretations differ. Source B supports the idea that Germans were attracted to the regime for different reasons and that it wasn't all due to fear and the use of terror.

Question 3(d): Evaluating interpretations

Question 3(d) on your exam paper will ask you to evaluate an interpretation by explaining how far you agree with it. There are 16 marks available for this question. An additional 4 marks are available for good spelling, punctuation, grammar (SPaG) and use of historical terminology.

Worked example

Links For more information, see pages 16, 20, 23, 25, 27 and 28.

How far do you agree with Interpretation 2 on page 37 about German public support for the Nazis?

Explain your answer, using both interpretations and your knowledge of the historical context.

(16 marks plus 4 marks for SPaG and use of specialist terminology)

How far do you agree?

You must:

✓ give detail from the interpretation to show that you understand the author's view

✓ provide detail from the historical context that supports the author's view

✓ consider how the interpretation is supported or challenged by the other interpretation and your own knowledge

✓ reach a judgement, giving reasons, about how far you agree with the view in the interpretation named in the question.

Sample extract

The view in the interpretation is that many Germans cooperated with the Gestapo and so most Germans must have supported the Nazis. I don't agree with this because they had to use concentration camps to get rid of opposition, and terror and propaganda to control people. The public didn't support the Nazis fully because there was opposition like the Edelweiss Pirates, so not everyone thought they should help them.

The student shows some understanding of the view in Interpretation 2 but needs to identify the interpretation more clearly.

Improved extract

Rees's view in Interpretation 2 is that the Gestapo were only effective because of information supplied to them by ordinary Germans, and I agree with this. However, I don't agree that this showed support for the Nazi regime. There could be many reasons why people cooperated with the Gestapo. Rees himself points out that the informants were ordinary Germans, not Nazi Party members.

The perception of the Gestapo as all-knowing and all-seeing was part of the carefully constructed image of the Nazi state, however cooperation with the Gestapo could be evidence that Germans were fearful of not appearing to support the regime and felt under pressure to 'name names'.

Rees portrays the Gestapo as an organisation dependent upon ordinary Germans, but Interpretation 1 challenges this view to some extent by saying that the Gestapo had fully penetrated German society. Delarue also refers to intimidation, which could have made it seem as though the German people supported the Gestapo and, linked to this, the Nazi regime.

The student makes valid points but doesn't give enough supporting evidence, and the line of argument is not well chosen because the Edelweiss Pirates were not typical of Germany as a whole.

Highlighting key points in the interpretation can help you focus on the precise arguments that you need to evaluate to make your judgement.

The student evaluates different points made in Interpretation 2, putting the arguments in the wider context, and goes on to challenge Interpretation 2 by bringing in Interpretation 1.

Remember that for this question an additional 4 marks are available for good spelling, grammar, punctuation and use of historical terminology. Use specific historical vocabulary, such as Gestapo, informants, perception, regime, intimidation.

Sources/Interpretations Booklet

These sources and interpretations are referred to in the worked examples on pages 31–36.

Source B: From an interview with a member of the Nazi Party, 1936

…for five years I remained unemployed and I was broken both in body and spirit and I learned how stupid were all my dreams in those hard days at university. I was not wanted by Germany… then I was introduced to Hitler. You won't understand and I cannot explain either because I don't know what happened, but life for me took on a tremendous new significance… I committed myself, body, soul and spirit, to the movement.

Source C: A poster produced by the Nazi Party in 1932, in which they appeal to women to support Hitler in the best interests of their family.

Interpretation 1: From *The History of the Gestapo*, by Jacques Delarue, published in 1964.

Never before, in no other land and at no time had an organisation attained such a comprehensive penetration of society, possessed such power and reached such a degree of...terror and horror, as well as...effectiveness. The Gestapo spotted or overheard every German's slightest movement.

Interpretation 2: From *The Nazis: A Warning from History*, by Laurence Rees, published in 2001.

Like all modern policing systems, the Gestapo was only as good or bad as the cooperation it received – and the files reveal that it received a high level of cooperation. Only around 10% of political crimes committed... were actually discovered by the Gestapo; another 10% were passed on to the Gestapo by the regular police or the Nazi Party. Around 80% was discovered by ordinary citizens who turned the information over... Most of this unpaid cooperation came from people who were not members of the Nazi Party – they were 'ordinary' citizens.

Practice

Put your skills and knowledge into practice with the following question.

Option 31: Weimar and Nazi Germany 1918–1939

SECTION A

Answer questions 1 and 2.

Source A: From a 1932 Nazi Party election flyer written to directly appeal to those supporting the Communist Party at the election.

> We Nazis help each other.
>
> He who has something to eat shares it with him who has nothing. He who has a spare bed gives it to him who has none. That is why we have become so strong. The election shows what we can do. Everyone helps! Everyone sacrifices! The unemployed give up their wedding rings. Everyone gives, even if it is but a penny. Many small gifts become a large one.

1 Give **two** things you can infer from Source A about Hitler's election tactics in Germany in the early 1930s.

Complete the table below to explain your answer. **(4 marks)**

(i) What I can infer:

Guided The Nazis used flyers to build support in the 1932
....
election
....

....

Details in the source that tell me this:

....

....

....

(ii) What I can infer:

....

....

....

Details in the source that tell me this:

....

....

....

....

You have 1 hour 20 minutes for the **whole** of Paper 3, so you should use the time carefully to answer all the questions fully. Remember to leave 5 minutes or so to check your work when you've finished writing.

Links You can revise Hitler's election tactics on page 13.

To 'infer' is to make a claim based on evidence, in this case, the source you are given in the exam.

Spend 5 minutes on this answer. You need to identify **two** valid inferences from the source.

An example of a suitable inference might be that 'The Nazis were specifically targeting certain groups like the communists who they saw as a group of voters they needed to win over to their ideas. I know this from the source because...'

You need to give supporting details selected from the source to back up both your inferences.

Practice

Put your skills and knowledge into practice with the following question.

2 Explain why the Nazis attempted the Munich Putsch in 1923.
  You may use the following in your answer:
  • invasion of the Ruhr (1923)
  • Hitler's leadership of the Nazi Party.
  You **must** also use information of your own.   (12 marks)

> **Guided** There are a number of causes behind the Nazis'
> attempt to seize power in 1923

....

....

....

....

....

....

....

....

....

....

....

....

....

....

....

....

....

....

....

....

....

....

....

....

You have 1 hour 20 minutes for the **whole** of Paper 3, so spend about 15 minutes on this answer.

'Explain' means you have to give causes of the Munich Putsch, not just describe what happened.

You need to include information of your own that is not in the bullet point hints.

⌒Links You can revise the Munich Putsch on page 11.

Marks are awarded for your analysis and understanding of causation and for your knowledge and understanding of the topic.

Useful phrases when answering causation questions include: because, led to, resulted in, propagated, factors that caused.

Keep your explanations focused on the question. Although you might remember lots of detail about the Munich Putsch, you need to focus on providing reasons why the Nazis attempted the Putsch, not on giving a description of it.

Practice

Use this page to continue your answer to question 2.

....
....
....
....
....
....
....
....
....
....
....
....
....
....
....
....
....
....
....
....
....
....
....
....
....
....
....

You need to show a good knowledge of the key features and characteristics of the event and analyse causation. You also need to show how factors combined to bring about an outcome – in this case, how different factors came to together, resulting in the Putsch.

Practice

Use this page to continue your answer to question 2.

....

....

....

....

....

....

....

....

....

....

....

....

....

....

....

....

....

....

....

....

....

....

....

....

....

Ending with a conclusion will help you to tie your analysis of the different factors back to the question.

Practice

Put your skills and knowledge into practice with the following question.

SECTION B

3 (a) Study Sources B and C on page 50.

How useful are Sources B and C for an enquiry into the ideas and tactics of the Nazi Party up to 1930?

Explain your answer, using Sources B and C and your knowledge of the historical context.   **(8 marks)**

Guided   Both sources B and C are useful for finding out

about Nazi ideas and tactics in the 1920s

....

....

....

....

....

....

....

....

....

....

....

....

....

....

....

....

....

....

....

....

....

....

....

....

You should spend about 10 minutes on this answer.

How useful means you have to judge what the sources suggest about the enquiry question and what the limits or problems could be.

Links You can revise Hitler's ideas and tactics on page 10.

You need to identify and comment on the pros and cons of each source and make a judgement.

Make sure you include some knowledge of the context and don't just rely on information given in the sources.

Practice

Use this page to continue your answer to question 3(a).

Guided However, there are some drawbacks with both sources for this enquiry. These include

....

....

....

Remember, you need to evaluate the usefulness of both sources.

....

....

....

....

....

....

....

....

....

....

....

....

....

....

....

....

....

....

....

....

....

....

....

....

....

....

....

Practice

Put your skills and knowledge into practice with the following question.

3 (b) **Study Interpretations 1 and 2 on page 51. They give different views about Nazi tactics and support up to 1930.**

What is the main difference between these views?

Explain your answer, using details from both interpretations. **(4 marks)**

You should spend about 7 minutes on this answer.

Guided Interpretations 1 and 2 both discuss Hitler's

tactics and support in the 1920s but offer different views.

....

....

....

....

....

....

....

....

....

....

....

🔗 **Links** You can revise Nazi support and tactics on page 12.

You need to identify the key difference, rather than just surface differences.

Make sure you refer to both the interpretations.

Remember, historians' interpretations are **their** views and opinions about causes, events and significance.

Remember to focus on the underlying **difference**.

Practice

Put your skills and knowledge into practice with the following question.

3 (c) Suggest **one** reason why Interpretations 1 and 2 on page 51 give different views about the Nazi tactics and support up to 1930.

You may use Sources B and C on page 50 to help explain your answer.   **(4 marks)**

You should spend about 6 minutes on this answer.

You need to explain **one** reason why the interpretations differ.

Guided   Interpretations 1 and 2 offer different views

about Nazi tactics and support because ....

....

....

....

....

....

....

....

....

....

....

You can revise how to analyse interpretations on page 30.

Focus on **why** the views are different. Think about whether the historians are giving different weight to different sources, whether they are using incomplete extracts, or if they have a different emphasis or focus.

Make sure you refer to **both** the interpretations to back up your answer.

Remember, historians' interpretations are **their** views and opinions about causes, events and significance.

Practice

Put your skills and knowledge into practice with the following question.

Up to 4 marks of the total will be awarded for spelling, punctuation, grammar and use of specialist terminology.

3 (d) How far do you agree with Interpretation 2 on page 51 about Hitler's tactics and support up to 1930?

Explain your answer, using both interpretations and your knowledge of the historical context.　　**(20 marks)**

Guided　I .... with the views in interpretation 2

....

....

....

....

....

....

....

....

....

....

....

....

....

....

....

....

....

....

....

....

....

....

....

....

....

....

You should spend about 30 minutes on this answer.

You can revise how to analyse interpretations on page 30.

You need to provide a clear line of argument. Say whether you agree or disagree in the first sentence.

Say why you think the interpretation is valid or questionable.

Remember that 4 marks are for **SPaG** in this question. Make sure you leave time to check your spelling, punctuation and grammar.

Make sure you refer clearly to your **own knowledge** of the **historical context**.

Practice

Use this page to continue your answer to question 3(d).

....
....
....
....
....
....
....
....
....
....
....
....
....
....
....
....
....
....
....
....
....
....
....
....
....
....
....
....
....
....
....
....
....
....

Remember, historians' interpretations offer **their** views for you to challenge.

Make sure you refer to both the interpretations to back up your answer.

Include a number of reasons for your opinion to build an argument throughout.

Practice

Use this page to continue your answer to question 3(d).

....

....

....

....

....

....

....

....

....

....

....

....

....

....

....

....

....

....

....

....

....

....

....

....

Practice

Use this page to continue your answer to question 3(d).

....
....
....
....   Include a brief conclusion to
....   sum up your argument.
....
....
....
....
....
....
....
....
....
....
....
....
....
....
....
....
....
....
....
....
....
....
....
....
....
....

Sources/Interpretations
Booklet 1

Sources/interpretations for use with the Section B questions on pages 42–49.

Source B: From the Twenty-Five Point Programme, originally produced by the DAP in February, 1920.

1. We demand the union of all Germans in a Greater Germany.
2. We demand equality of rights for the German people in its dealings with other nations.
3. We demand land and colonies to feed our people and settle our surplus population.
4. Only those of German blood... are members of the nation. No Jew may be a member of the nation.
7. We demand that the State's primary duty must be to promote work and the livelihood of its citizens.
9. All citizens shall have equal rights and equal duties.
17. We demand... a law to take from the owners any land needed for the common good of the people.
22. We demand... the creation of a people's army.
25. We demand the creation of a strong central state power for the Reich.

Source C: A NSDAP campaign poster from 1924. It emphasises Nazi principles of family, work and nationalism.

Sources/Interpretations Booklet 2

Sources/interpretations for use with Section B questions on pages 42–49.

Interpretation 1: From *The Hitler Myth*, by Ian Kershaw, published in *History Today* Volume 35 Issue 11, November 1985.

> Before 1930, the… Führer cult around Hitler found an echo among at most a few hundred thousand followers. But with the Nazi Party's breakthrough in the 1930 election (which brought it 18.3 per cent of the vote), the Führer cult ceased to be merely the property of a fanatical fringe party. The potential was there for its massive extension, as more and more Germans saw in Nazism – symbolised by its leader – the only hope for a way out of gathering crisis. Those now surging to join the Nazi Party were often already willing victims of the 'Hitler Myth'. Not untypical was the new party member who wrote that after hearing Hitler speak for the first time, 'there was only one thing for me, either to win with Adolf Hitler or to die for him. The personality of the Führer had me totally in its spell'. Even for the vast majority of the German people who did not share such sentiments, there was the growing feeling – encouraged by Hitler's profile even in the non-Nazi press – that Hitler was not just another politician, that he was a party leader extraordinary, a man towards whom one could not remain neutral.

Interpretation 2: From *The Coming of the Third Reich*, by Richard J Evans, published in 2004.

> Nazi propaganda… skilfully targeted specific groups in the German electorate… providing topics for particular venues and picking the speaker to fit the occasion. The… Party recognized the growing divisions of German society into competing interest groups in the course of the Depression and tailored their message to their particular constituency. The Nazis adapted… a whole range of posters and leaflets designed to win over different parts of the electorate.

Answers

Where an exemplar answer is given, this is not necessarily the only correct response. In most cases there is a range of responses that can gain full marks.

SUBJECT CONTENT
The Weimar Republic, 1918–29

1. The legacy of the First World War

Economic problems:

Fighting left two million troops dead and over four million wounded. Costs meant German government debts increased from 50 billion marks to 150 billion marks. Over 750 000 Germans died because of food shortages during the First World War. Germany started to fall apart from within before the war was over.

Political problems:

The Kaiser fled to Holland after the army and his ministers withdrew their support. The Kaiser abdicated and Ebert became chancellor and a republic was declared on 9 November. There was a lot of unrest on the streets and the new leaders were keen to make sure the transition to the republic was peaceful. On 11 November the armistice was signed. It was the first big decision of Ebert's new German government. Germany was forced to sign this as the country was rapidly being destroyed and faced mass social and political unrest.

2. Strengths and weaknesses of the Weimar Constitution

For example:

I feel the main strength of the Weimar Constitution was that more people could vote: this now included everyone, men and women, over the age of 21. The greatest weakness was Article 48, which allowed the President to pass laws without the prior consent of the Reichstag.

3. Why the Republic was unpopular

For example:

Very unfair treaty terms
Everyone in Germany criticised the terms
Revealed weaknesses in the support for the
Socialists who were forced to sign the terms
Alsace Lorraine returned to France along with other lost territories
Instalments of compensation paid to the Allies
Little effort made to reconcile with Germany
Let them accept the blame for starting the war
Easy to force them to accept war guilt
Stabbed in the back

4. Challenges from left and right

The Freikorps were sent by the Weimar government to put down the Spartacist Revolt in Berlin, in 1919. This led to street fighting. In March 1920, the Freikorps marched on Berlin in protest, fearing that they would become unemployed. The government asked the army to stop the Freikorps but the head of the army refused and the Weimar government fled from Berlin. The Freikorps put a nationalist politician, Dr Kapp, in charge. The government persuaded the trade unions to go on strike. This caused chaos and made it impossible for Kapp to run Germany, so he fled and the Weimar government returned to Berlin.

5. The challenges of 1923

For example:

- Pensions became worthless. Those affected included the elderly and war widows.
- Savings became worthless. Those affected included the middle-classes because they were more likely to have savings. However, people with mortgages and loans benefited, as they could now pay them off. Businesses with loans also benefited, and some of these businesses took over other businesses that were struggling.
- Fixed rents became cheaper. Those who benefited included people who rented rooms or shops.
- Wages didn't rise as quickly as inflation. This reduced the value of workers' wages.
- Higher price of food. This benefited farmers, because they were paid higher sums for their products.
- For example, the price of raw materials, parts rose. Some businesses went bankrupt. This affected workers and the people who owned the businesses.

6. Reasons for recovery, 1923–29

The crisis of 1923 was resolved in the short term but Germany was now very reliant on American loans. The problem with this was that, if in the future America faced economic difficulties, Germany would experience the knock-on effect. Also, extreme political parties were against paying any reparations, which meant they were very hostile and wanted the democratic system to fail.

7. Stresemann's success at home and abroad

By making sure Germany was part of the Locarno Pact, the League of Nations and the Kellogg-Briand Pact, Stresemann increased Germany's position and confidence internationally, which helped to stabilise the country.

8. Changes for workers and women

For example, for workers:

Progress – There was unemployment insurance for the poor if they lost their jobs or were ill.

Lack of progress – Resentment of wealthier Germans towards improvements for poorer members of society.

For example, for women:

Progress – Greater independence for younger, single women because of their greater earning power.

Lack of progress – Women's position in society returned to the inequality of the pre-war years.

9. Cultural changes, 1924–29

The Weimar culture challenged traditional values in Germany through art, cinema and architecture. The main movement that affected these three areas was Expressionism, which was concerned with raw emotion. Artists explored the seedier side of everyday life, architects used radical new approaches, designing buildings that were very different to traditional German styles, and films were dramatic and had grotesque characters, a style of film making that had not been seen before.

Hitler's rise to power, 1919–33

10. Hitler and the early growth of the party

For example:

1 Get rid of the Treaty of Versailles: this had wide appeal as it was hated by many as an unfair punishment. They particularly despised the war guilt clause and the associated payments for reparations.

2 Increase pensions for the elderly: this would have appealed to the elderly because it would give them security in retirement.

3 Build up Germany's armed forces: popular with those who wanted to make Germany a great nation and played on people's sense of national pride and patriotism.

11. The Munich Putsch and its aftermath

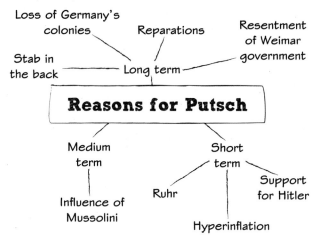

12. Growth in support, 1929–32

Rise of Nazis	Weimar problems
• The depression led to mass unemployment, which allowed the Nazis to get their message across. • Hitler promised to restore law and order. • Hitler was popular and featured on their posters, and travelled the country to make election speeches. • The Nazis had support from wealthy businessmen, which gave Hitler funding for the costs of running for election and appealed to all sectors of society in one way or another. • The uniformed SA made the Nazis seem strong. • The SA disrupted opposition from other political parties.	• Many Germans were unhappy with the Weimar Republic. • The Weimar government was weak and had not solved the economic problems. • The government refused to print more money for fear of creating an inflation crisis like that of 1923. • The government cut unemployment benefit, which was unpopular.

13. Political developments in 1932

1 and 2 For example (from least to most important):

1 Hitler made promises that some Germans wanted to hear.

2 Hitler was underestimated.

3 Hitler had significant support and secured more votes than other parties, despite not gaining a majority.

4 Other politicians thought they could use Hitler as a figurehead to manipulate him and improve their positions of power.

5 Powerful people in Germany, like Hindenburg, were keen to stop the communists or a military dictatorship, so Hitler seemed to be an alternative that would stop this happening.

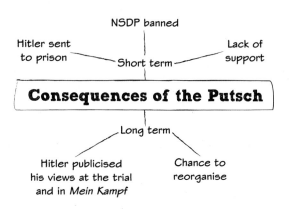

Nazi dictatorship, 1933–39

14. The Reichstag Fire and the Enabling Act, 1933

On 27 February 1933, the Reichstag building was set ablaze. The Nazis presented the fire as an attack on the political system. The Nazis blamed the communists for the arson attack claiming that they were seeking to undermine the Nazis and wanted to destroy the heart of the German government. On hearing the news Hitler instructed the SA to be vigilant in case of further communist violence.

Hitler said he would show the necessary strength and offer no mercy to those who were found guilty of these acts that he said were treason against the people of Germany. The Enabling Act was passed in March 1933 and gave Hitler the power to pass laws without the approval of the Reichstag. Hitler argued it was a necessary law to protect Germany in the light of the Reichstag Fire. Van der Lubbe, a communist, was arrested and found guilty of the Reichstag attack. He was executed in January 1934 for the crime.

15. Hitler becomes Führer

Hitler took a series of steps to secure the dictatorship in 1934. On June 30, Hitler orchestrated the Night of the Long Knives, during which those who threatened to oppose the Nazi Party from within were murdered. Then, in August, after the death of Hindenburg, he passed a law to merge the roles of Chancellor and President, and to create a new position as Führer. Finally, he made the army swear a personal oath of allegiance to him, rather than to the country.

16. A police state

For example:

1 The SS controlled Germany's police and security forces.
2 The SS acted outside the law and arrested potential opposition.
3 The SS ran the concentration camps.

17. Policies towards the churches

Ways that the churches cooperated:

- The Catholic Church signed the concordat.
- The Reich Church supported the Nazis and its members called themselves German Christians.
- Reich churches were well attended.

Ways that the churches resisted:

- In 1937, the pope issued 'With burning anxiety', which criticised the Nazis.
- Some individuals spoke out and were punished.
- In 1934, some protestants broke away and set up the Confessional Church to secure more independence from Nazi control.

18. Propaganda and censorship

Workers – Loudspeakers broadcast in factories and cafés repeated the Nazi messages.

Women – Art that presented the traditional family and valued women as mothers was encouraged.

Young people – Cinema showed propaganda films containing the Nazi message.

19. Church opposition

Hitler's ultimate aim was to gain complete control over the churches in Germany. However, there was some opposition to his ambition. Although the churches were initially willing to accept Hitler as a political leader of Germany and even welcomed some of his ideas, as time went on some people were willing to oppose him. Martin Niemöller is a good example of this change. Niemöller, and others like him in the Confessional Church, were willing to allow Hitler political power, but objected when the Nazis tried to interfere in matters of faith and their church practices. They wanted religious autonomy and when this was threatened they were willing to stand up against Hitler's government.

20. Youth opposition

For example:

- Listening to banned music.
- Organising political resistance.
- Attacking members of the Hitler Youth.

Life in Nazi Germany, 1933–39

21. Women and the family

- In Weimar Germany women were allowed to have a job; in Nazi Germany, women were expected to have large families instead of working.
- In Weimar Germany, women were encouraged to attend university; in Nazi Germany university places were restricted.
- In Weimar Germany women were free to go out and enjoy themselves; during the Nazi period they were expected to stay at home and not drink or smoke.

22. Nazi youth organisations

Hitler wanted to control what young people did at all times, in school and outside it. Youth organisations were a good way of doing this and gave him the opportunity to train boys and girls in the skills he felt were important, such as military skills for boys and domestic skills for girls. It was also a good way of teaching young people Nazi policies and attitudes.

23. Nazi education

The Nazis had different aims for boys and girls: they wanted boys to be taught skills that would be useful in their future career as soldiers; girls were taught skills that were useful for becoming mothers and looking after the home.

24. Policies to reduce unemployment

The Nazi employment policies benefited people who worked in armaments and construction. The policies didn't benefit those people the Nazis didn't like, for example, the Jewish community, whose jobs the Nazis took away. The policies also didn't help women, who were expected to stay at home rather than work. Also affected were men under 25: they had to do National Labour Service, where pay was poor and hours were long.

25. The standard of living

Standard of living had improved:

Unemployment fell very significantly from 4.8 million to 0.3 million by 1939. Nazi work organisations, such as the SdA, improved working conditions for workers. Strength through Joy organised leisure for workers.

Standard of living had not improved:

Workers rights were reduced with the banning of trade unions and an increase in hours worked per week. Unemployment numbers were manipulated by shifting people into public work schemes. Women who were unemployed were not counted and neither were minorities, like the Jews. The economic upturn after the severe depression is part of the economic cycle and not something for which Nazi economics can take all the credit.

26. Racial beliefs and policies

The Nazis described gypsies as Untermenschen and 'inferior' to the Aryan ideal. After 1933, the Nazis began to arrest gypsies and place them in concentration camps. After the Nuremberg Laws were passed, gypsies were no longer allowed to marry Aryans. As the decade wore on, the treatment of gypsies became harsher and their freedoms limited. In 1938, laws were passed to prevent any gypsy travelling and all gypsies had to be registered. Finally, in 1939, they were threatened with deportation, which meant they were told they had to leave the country.

27. Jewish persecution 1

Economic persecution – Jews were not allowed to inherit land. In 1933, the SA organised a boycott of Jewish shops, and in 1937 Jewish businesses were taken over by Aryans. Jews were blamed for Kristallnacht and fined 1 billion marks.

Social persecution – Jews were banned from public places such as parks and swimming pools. They were forced to add 'Israel' or 'Sarah' to their names to make them stand out. Jewish actors and musicians were not allowed to perform.

Open violence – During Kristallnacht, Jewish shops, homes, businesses and synagogues were set on fire or vandalised, and Jews were openly attacked and killed.

28. Jewish persecution 2

The treatment of Jews changed a lot over the first three years of Nazi rule. The boycott of shops and businesses was an attack on the living standards of Jews and was intended to isolate the Jewish community. By 1935, the Nuremberg Laws made it impossible for a Jew to be a German citizen. Also, the Marriage Law, in the name of creating the 'master race', stopped Jews and Aryans having relationships and children together. Kristallnacht also marked a change in the way the Nazis treated the Jews, becoming openly violent and hostile.

PRACTICE
38. Practice

1 The Nazis used flyers to build support in the 1932 election, from this I can infer that the Nazis deliberately targeted certain groups that they believed might be persuaded to vote for them.

Details in the source that tell me this are the fact it is a Nazi Party election flyer that sets out specific reasons why communists should change their allegiance and vote Nazi instead. For example, it says, "We Nazis help each other. He who has something to eat shares it with him who has nothing." Drawing attention to the socialist aspect of National Socialism was used to attract left-wing voters.

I can infer that, by 1932, the Nazis were seeking to use the election system to get power by being voted into office, rather than only using violent means.

Details in the source that tell me this are that issuing flyers was an opportunity to provide voters with clear ideas about what the Nazis stood for. The Nazis' hope was that voters would turn out and support them at the ballot box.

39. Practice

2 There are a number of causes behind the Nazis' attempt to seize power in 1923. These include Hitler's personal ambitions and ideas about how to get power. Also, the political and economic situation at the time seemed like it might give them the opportunity they were looking for.

The ideas of the Nazi Party were based on struggle and fighting for power, so they accepted violent uprising as an inevitable part of their rise to power. Hitler believed that the strongest would survive over weaker people in society. Hitler believed that Germany's problems were caused by weak leadership, and that's why he said Germany needed a strong army and to end the Treaty of Versailles.

The Nazis only had about 300 members in 1923 but he still believed they could start a revolution that would lead to him gaining power in Germany. The specific problems in 1923 meant Hitler thought the time was right. Stresemann had called off the passive resistance campaign. Many people were angry and saw this as yet another example of Germany being humiliated. Kahr, the head of the government in Bavaria, was right-wing and they wanted to see the end of the Weimar government. Hitler, therefore, believed that Kahr would support his Putsch.

Also, Hitler had built up a relationship with old army leaders like Ludendorff. Hitler believed that they could be called upon for support when the time came, and that the army would end their support for the government and turn to the Nazis instead.

So, overall, Hitler's philosophy, the belief that he would gain support from powerful individuals and groups in Germany, and a political and economic crisis, contributed to the Munich Putsch.

42. Practice

3 (a) Both sources B and C are useful for finding out about Nazi ideas and tactics in the 1920s. Source B is an extract from the Nazi Party Twenty-Five Point Programme. This is useful for finding out about their ideas and tactics because it is a document produced by them at the time stating their specific aims and vision for Germany. Source C is also useful for this enquiry as it is a poster produced by the Nazis at that time. It presents Nazi ideas about German families and the values they wanted to promote. It is very useful for showing Nazi tactics. Posters were an important aspect of how they campaigned to get support.

However, there are some drawbacks with both sources for this enquiry. These include the fact that this is what the Nazis wanted to present to the public and so it might be affected by how they wanted to portray their organisation. At that time, the Weimar Republic had lots of people who criticised them so the Nazis wanted to appear strong and willing to pick up causes that might get them support, like focusing on people's basic needs for work and food. Source B was produced by the Nazi Party and so we must consider how they wanted their organisation's aims to come across. Source C is also limited as its focus is limited to the role of women and families and does not reveal much about Nazi ideas and tactics more generally.

44. Practice

3 (b) Interpretations 1 and 2 both discuss Hitler's tactics and support in the 1920s but offer different views. Evans claims Nazi support resulted from its propaganda tactics. He argues that the Nazis were skilled at targeting different interest groups with specific messages that appealed to them and that this led to their support growing. On the other hand, Kershaw claims that 1930 marked a 'breakthrough', because the 'Hitler Myth' meant that the power of Hitler's cult of personality was expanded to the electorate more generally, rather than to just his 'fanatical' followers.

45. Practice

3 (c) Interpretations 1 and 2 offer different views about Nazi tactics and support because they have different focuses.

Kershaw, in interpretation 1, focuses on Hitler's personal appeal, even for those who were not natural Nazi supporters, and his ability to create a 'Führer cult'.

In contrast, Evans, in interpretation 2, emphasises the impact of Nazi propaganda, tactics and election strategy, and how these led to increased support. Source C, which depicts the Nazi principles of family, work and nationalism, helps to explain Evans' view, as it shows the power of Nazi propaganda in trying to establish support for its ideas.

46. Practice

3 (d) I agree with the views in interpretation 2 to quite an extent. It is true that the Nazis were skilled at targeting a range of different groups and adjusting their message accordingly. For example, their slogans included 'work and bread' to attract working-class votes. On the other hand, they campaigned saying 'smash Versailles' to appeal to nationalist-minded voters who still resented the outcome of the First World War. In interpretation 2, Evans argues that the Nazis adapted their message during the course of the economic depression in order to capitalise on the bad effects the crisis was having on the German people.

However, a limitation of the argument in interpretation 2 is that it does not take account of the personal attraction that Hitler managed to construct. As Kershaw argues in interpretation 1, Hitler managed to create a personality cult. Kershaw claims that even those German voters who did not share Hitler's 'sentiments' accepted that he was not like any ordinary politician.

Interpretation 2 on the other hand, does examine some of the ways in which the Nazi tactics gained support. Evans acknowledges that the Nazis were good at using divisions in Germany to get votes. He also points out the importance of Hitler's messages, and how these were adapted for different audiences and interest groups, like the young or workers. He says their tactics and messages were 'skilfully' deployed.

Therefore, I agree with interpretation 2 that the use of different tactics was important to increase Nazi support. Hitler and Goebbels understood that propaganda needed to be targeted at specific audiences and this was vital in their increased popularity at elections. However, Kershaw's arguments in interpretation 1 about the significance of the 'Hitler Myth' helps explain the dramatic increases in the Nazi share of the vote in the 1932 election as he was indeed presented as superhuman and the saviour of the German people.

Notes

Notes

Notes

Notes

Notes

Published by Pearson Education Limited, 80 Strand, London, WC2R 0RL.

www.pearsonschoolsandfecolleges.co.uk

Copies of official specifications for all Pearson qualifications may be found on the website: qualifications.pearson.com

Text and illustrations © Pearson Education Limited 2017
Produced, typeset and illustrated by Tech-Set, Ltd
Cover illustration by Eoin Coveney
Picture Research by Alison Prior

The right of Victoria Payne to be identified as author of this work has been asserted by her in accordance with the Copyright, Designs and Patents Act 1988.

Content written by Rob Bircher, Brian Dowse and Kirsty Taylor is included.

First published 2017

20 19

10

British Library Cataloguing in Publication Data
A catalogue record for this book is available from the British Library

ISBN 978 1 292 16973 6

Acknowledgements
The publisher would like to thank the following for their kind permission to reproduce their photographs:

(Key: b-bottom; c-centre; l-left; r-right; t-top)

akg-images Ltd: 9cl, 10, 12tr; **Alamy Images**: A F Archive 18tl, Chronicle 5, Everett Collection Historical 8l, Hi-Story 18br, / Keystone Pictures USA 18c, Lebrecht Music and Arts Photo Library 4, Mary Evans Picture Library 24, Pictorial Press Ltd 2, 13 (Hindenburg), Terry Mathews 20bc, World History Archive 20t, 21, 28br; **Bridgeman Art Library Ltd**: Nazi propaganda poster featuring Adolf Hitler, 1938 (colour litho), German School, (20th century) / Private Collection / Peter Newark Military Pictures / Bridgeman Images 18cl, SZ Photo / Scherl 16; **Getty Images**: 545961347 12tl, Albert Harlingue 8c, Bettmann 19, Bob Thomas / Popperfoto 31, Heritage Images 37, Iain Masterton 9bc, Keystone 11, Keystone France 15, Three Lions 8r, ullstein bild 13 (von Papen), 13 (von Schleicher); **Mary Evans Picture Library**: 50, Imago 12cl, Rubert Hunt Library 1bl, Sueddeutsche Zeitung Photo 3, 6, 17, 27, SZ Photo / Scherl 9c, 25tl, 25cl, WEIMAR ARCHIVE 1c, 13 (Bruning), 14, 26, 28tr

All other images © Pearson Education

We are grateful to the following for permission to reproduce copyright material:

Text
Interview on page 37 from *Hitler and Nazism*, Longman (Jenkins, Jane 1998), Pearson Education Limited; Extract on page 37 from *The History of the Gestapo*, Macdonald & Co (Delarue, J. 1964), Frontline Books/Pen and Sword Books Reprinted by permission of Skyhorse Publishing, Inc; Extract on page 37 from *The Nazis: A Warning from History* Copyright © 1999 by Laurence Rees. Reprinted by permission of The New Press. www.thenewpress.com; Extract on page 38 from *Nazi party election flyer*, copyright 1999 by Randall L. Bytwerk. German Propaganda Archive, Calvin College4; Extract on page 51 from THE COMING OF THE THIRD REICH by Richard J. Evans (Penguin Books 2003). Copyright © Richard Evans 2003., Used by permission of Penguin Press, an imprint of Penguin and Publishing Group, a division of Penguin Random House LLC. All rights reserved.; Extract on page 51 from *The Hitler Myth*, History Today (Kershaw, I 1985) Volume 35, issue 11, November 1985., Used by permission of the copyright holder, History Today Ltd.